MW01400504

AL-GHAZĀLĪ

The Mysteries of Purification for Children

Imam al-Ghazali
The Book on the Mysteries of Purity
for Children

To the Prophet Muhammad ﷺ
and
his family
we humbly dedicate this effort.

Imam al-Ghazali
The Book on the
Mysteries of Purity
for Children
Book Three from the
Ihya Ulum al-Din

FONS VITAE

The Book on the Mysteries of Purity For Children

For the dear soul of blessed Soumayya Aatek

First published in 2017 by
Fons Vitae
49 Mockingbird Valley Drive
Louisville, KY 40207
http://www.fonsvitae.com
Email: fonsvitaeky@aol.com

© 2017 Fons Vitae
No part of this book may be reproduced
in any form without prior permission of
the publishers. All rights reserved.

Library of Congress Control Number: 2017948507

ISBN 978-1941610-336

Printed in Canada

Illustrations by Mary Minifie

Reviewed by Dr. Ingrid Mattson, Shaykh Walead Mosaad, Prof. Zeinab Keeler, Dr. Homaira Wassel, and Arzina Ali.

Please frequent www.ghazalichildren.org for updates, competitions, meeting one another and much more.

The decorative tree motif used throughout was found on a carved panel in Nishapur, and might have been seen by Imam al-Ghazali when he studied in that Persian city during the 11th century.

Table of Contents

Foreword	7
Introduction by Shaykh Hamza Yusuf	9
Opening Passage from The Book on the Mysteries of Purity	15
The Book of Purity Prologue	17
Chapter One: What Is *Wudu*?	21
Chapter Two: The Four Levels of Purification: Cleansing and Purifying Oneself	27
Chapter Three: The Magical Tree House and the Levels of Faith	33
Chapter Four: Back in the Special Meeting Place	41
Chapter Five: Some Parts of Outward Purity	47
Chapter Six: Washing With Water	51
Chapter Seven: The Toothbrush	55
Chapter Eight: How to Begin *Wudu*: The Mouth	59
Chapter Nine: The Nose	63
Chapter Ten: The Brightened Face	65
Chapter Eleven: Shining Hands and Forearms	69
Chapter Twelve: The Top of The Head and The Neck	71
Chapter Thirteen: Finally, Your Feet	75
Chapter Fourteen: More Helpful Information	79
Chapter Fifteen: Breakfast at Grandmother's	83
Chapter Sixteen: In What Way Should We Try to Look Beautiful?	89
Chapter Seventeen: The Order in Which We Do Things	93

The Book on the Mysteries of Purity For Children

بسم الله الرحمن الرحيم

Foreword

Dear Children,

Now that you have learned some ways to polish your heart from the *Book of Knowledge* and also about what happens to us after death from the *Book of Belief*, when we are responsible and accountable for how we have used our lives in this world, we turn to this essential book which will help you to better understand the importance and the meaning of purity.

Your parents and family will teach you much of what you need to know about this special purity according to your age as you grow up, and will give you additional details. What we are giving you here, from Imam al-Ghazali's third book of the *Revival of the Religious Sciences*, are some of the inner meanings of purity which you will find fascinating and useful. What he explains will greatly help all of you in your noble effort to polish your beautiful, shining hearts.

There is available on your own special website, ghazalichildren.org, a link for youth which presents further details from Imam al-Ghazali's *Book on the Mysteries of Purity*, intended for teenagers.

One of the beauties of Islamic law is that there are many acceptable ways to perform certain rites. There are variations for the performance of *wudu* in the different Islamic schools of law throughout the Islamic world, such as the Maliki, Hanifi, Hanbali, and Shafi'i.

Again, these are outer differences but the inward *sunna* is

The Book on the Mysteries of Purity For Children

what we are mostly aiming to learn in this wonderful book from Imam al-Ghazali.

In the stories you are reading, the special teacher is called Haj Abdullah, who like his name, has made the Pilgrimage, the journey to the sacred center and performed all that is required. Abdullah means that he truly serves God.

In the books and workbooks of this Series, we have shown Haj Abdullah in different ways – he sometimes appears old and at other times younger. The country he seems to come from varies as well. The reason is: Haj Abdullah *could* be your own grandfather or some family member. He *could* be an imam or a teacher or a wise elder. You can find the fine character of Haj Abdullah in many respected grown ups in your very own communities!

Haj Abdullah is found everywhere at all times and in everyplace. Does he remind you of Imam al-Ghazali whose teachings he is passing on to you? Do you think the way he is, as a person, shows that he is practicing all the things the Imam recommends – things he learned about from reading Quran and *hadith*? Who do you know that has his beautiful, peaceful qualities, as well as his helpful, loving, and wise nature? Hopefully as you grow up you will teach by copying his way of being completely present to anyone he is with. The greatest gifts we can give one another are our complete presence and pure, shining hearts.

Introduction
Wudu Means "What Makes You Shine."
by Shaykh Hamza Yusuf

Your life is a miracle. Everything about you is amazing. You are unique, and no one in the world is exactly like you. But did you know you are seventy percent water? That means that if you weighed one hundred pounds, then seventy of them would be water! The surface of the earth that you live on is also seventy percent water and thirty percent land, just like you. The rest of the materials that make up your body are from the earth. You have calcium, magnesium, phosphates, silica, and many other minerals in your body. You are a little earth. And God made you so that good things could grow from you: good fruits that we call good deeds.

The Quran tells us that God made us from water and clay. Every part of the earth's surface was used to make us, which is why we have all these different colors among people: brown, black, yellow, red, white, and various other hues or colors. God made us from the topsoil of the earth, and the earth has all of these colors. Along with the earth, we were also made with water. Water is the basis for life. No life can exist without water. The Quran says, "And We created from water every living thing." When scientists look at other planets to see if there is life on them, they first see if there is water.

Water is wondrous, isn't it? Have you ever thought about how we can swim in it even though it is a completely different substance than air? Our bodies are designed to move in air and water. We can't move in rocks or vegetation without bumping into them, unless we cut through the rock by making a tunnel

The Book on the Mysteries of Purity For Children

or the vegetation by making a path or a road. But our bodies can wade or swim through water, while we don't even notice the air we walk through every day.

Water is made up of two elements, which are the building blocks of our world: hydrogen and oxygen. In science, water is called H_2O, which means there are two parts hydrogen and one part oxygen. Most of our universe is made up of hydrogen atoms. Guess what is the atomic number of hydrogen. If you guessed one, then you're right! One is everywhere. Water, even though it is made up of lots of atoms, is *one* thing.

All of the world, including water, points to One. Everything comes from One, and that One has many signs to point to Him. God hides from us so that we seek Him out. He wants us to find Him, and so He has left lots of clues to make it exciting for us. Water is one of those clues. God sends rain down to the earth and brings it back to life. God tells us in the Quran that "Just like we bring a dead earth to life with rain, you will be brought back to life after you die." Water is what we use to clean ourselves from dirty things. When you play in the park, sometimes you get dirty from the earth, which is good for you; your clothes get dirty too. When you get home, you wash to remove the dirt, and your mom or dad washes your clothes for you. Well, did you know that people get dirty inside too? They get dirty not by physical dirt that you find outside but by a different dirt that harms our souls.

What kind of dirt is that? Well, it comes from doing or intending bad things. For instance, when we tell a story that is not true. Have you ever done that? You, like most people, probably have. Did you feel bad? Of course you did, because your soul is speaking to you and telling you that what you did was wrong. That feeling is from God to remind you that you need to clean yourself.

Now, how do you clean that unseen dirt? God gave us our heart and water to do this. The heart is the place where you feel you did something wrong, and also the place where you make intentions. For example, when you say to yourself, "I'm never going to do that again." Water is what you use for *wudu* or *ghusl*. When you're little, you don't have to do *ghusl* as it's only for adults. *Wudu*, however, you need to learn now. In English, we have an old word for *wudu*; it's called lustration (some people call it ablution, but I like lustration). *Wudu,* in Arabic, means, "What makes you shine." Lustration is an old English word for ritual or religious washing before prayers, and it's related to luster, which means to shine! Have you noticed when you wash your face that sometimes it shines afterward? That's because you are taking away that unseen dirt. You were meant to shine, and you have a light in your face that grows with goodness and diminishes or gets weaker with wickedness.

When people are little, like you, they have no sins or wicked deeds, so they have a lot of light in their faces. Look at your baby brother or sister, if you have one, and notice the way their faces and eyes shine. That's because they are pure. They haven't any unseen dirt on them to wash away. But as people get older and learn right from wrong, they sometimes choose wrong and the light gets weaker. If they keep doing wrong, it gets weaker and weaker until it goes out. Those are called dark people, because they have no light. Many black people have lots of light in their faces from their good deeds and good character, while some white people have very dark faces from their bad deeds. So this is not black and white in color, but dark and light in the presence of good and evil.

The better a person is, no matter what color, the more light they have in their faces. The more evil they are, the less light they have in their faces. Some people, who are not very smart, make the mistake that it is about color; these people think because a person's skin color is lighter they are better. They don't understand that it is not color, but the light that glows in good faces regardless of whether they are black, brown, yellow, red, or white. Good people share that light, and there are good people in every skin color, just like there are bad people in every skin color. That's what God means in the Quran when He says, "On that day (meaning the day of judgment) some faces are white and some are black." He means white with light even if they are black in color, and black with no light even if they are white in color.

Black is an amazing color. In physics, which studies light among other things, black is the perfect absorber of light, which is why the pupil of your eye is black. People that have this color are lucky. They absorb sunlight better than people that don't, so they don't get sunburnt. This is important because some people don't understand this and treat people of different colors badly; they think spiritual light is a color or that spiritual darkness is a color. These are not colors; rather, they are states of being that are either good or bad.

God says about good people, "The sign of their goodness is in their faces." Look at your parent's beautiful faces. That is because they are good people who do good things and care deeply about you. God put lots of light in you, but you have to protect it with good. When you do a misdeed, you ask God to forgive you and then wash with water. This is why we wash with water before our prayers, because we want to be pure with no unseen dirt on our souls when we stand before God.

In this book that you are going to read, one of our greatest saints and teachers, Imam Abu Hamid al-Ghazali, is going to teach you about the secrets of purification with water. You will learn many things, but the most important is that our souls need washing regularly just like our bodies; we have to be clean inside and out. This is a very great knowledge that you are going to receive, but you must put it to use. Imam al-Ghazali once said, "Knowledge without action is insanity." Insanity means crazy, but the word in Latin means unclean. If we don't clean ourselves, it affects our minds in bad ways. Please make sure you practice what you learn. The Prophet said, peace be upon him, "Whoever practices what they learn, God will give them knowledge they didn't learn." So some knowledge is learned by study, but if you apply that in doing good, God gives you another knowledge that doesn't come from study. It is called wisdom. People that have this knowledge are called wise people, and Imam al-Ghazali was one of the wisest who ever lived. Now, it's time to learn from his wisdom about water.

The Book on the Mysteries of Purity For Children

Opening Passage from The Book on the Mysteries of Purity

Praise be to God Who, in Kindness to His servants, ordained cleanliness to be part of their worship, poured down upon their hearts His Lights and Graces to purify their souls, and made water limpid and gentle for the cleansing of their bodies.

May the blessings of God be upon Muhammad and his people, good and pure, by whom guidance flooded into the farthest reaches of the world, a blessing that will shelter us with its benediction on the Fearful day and be a shield between us and every calamity and disaster.

To proceed, the Prophet ﷺ said, "Religion (*din*) is built upon cleanliness."

...and also, "Purity (*tahara*) is the key to prayer."

And God most high says,

> *Within it are men who love to purify themselves, and God loves those who purify themselves* [9:108].

And the Prophet ﷺ also said, "Purification is half of faith,"

...and God most high says,

> *God does not intend to make difficulty for you, but He intends to purify you* [5:6]

The Book on the Mysteries of Purity For Children

Qasim blurted out, "Oh Haj Abdullah, truly our lives have been changed in a joyous way. Every day is now fun because whatever happens, whether difficult or not, we can see ways to understand it and use it to brighten our hearts!"

The Book of Purity
Prologue

The neighborhood children were amazed at finding such unexpected happiness in all that they were learning from their families, teachers, Haj Abdullah and the magical visits by Imam al-Ghazali. One afternoon, after school let out, they met Haj Abdullah with more questions about Real Learning and to further discuss what happens after death. In their special meeting place within the forgotten garden, they wanted to share an important and wondrous idea with their beloved teacher.

But first, Qasim blurted out, "Oh Haj Abdullah, truly our lives have been changed in a joyous way. Every day is now fun because whatever happens, whether difficult or not, we can see ways to understand it and use it to brighten our hearts!"

"And our lives!" added Maryam. "We are not so easily upset by silly things anymore. We love the Real Special Learning."

Yusuf added, "And finding out what happens when we die! We all wanted to know about that! It's good we don't have to worry so much anymore because now we have a plan, a super map from Imam al-Ghazali, that helps us use everything in our normal lives as children, to polish our real hearts. It makes everything that happens to us into a chance to do something *real*, and fun!"

Amina explained, "Oh respected teacher, Haj Abdullah, remember the story of the two trees and the many other tales in the *Book of Knowledge*? How the best thing we can do is share this new learning with others, and more than that, be living examples who put what we are learning into practice! The whales and ants ask God to bless good teachers! I love the idea of them praying for me!"

Haj Abdullah beamed with joy, "Now tell me, children! What wondrous idea did you wish to share with me?"

Yusuf replied, "We have been talking together and feel it is only right to include more of our school mates into our special gatherings."

Haj Abdullah said, "Excellent idea – but remember, it's not just about widening our group. What is most important is that you each *do* what you now know is best."

Qasim said, "I'll be honest. It's become very hard for me to speak badly about someone else now. Or listen to backbiting. I feel too uncomfortable."

Layla exclaimed, "Yes! I have stopped arguing a lot! And I am, believe it or not, learning to want the best for others. And it feels great! Once I started doing it, it became a habit; it makes me feel like the good person I truly am: my Real Self."

"Right!" continued Amina, "I am watching my lower false self. I keep catching myself saying 'ugly truths!' I will admit I want to be liked by people so I keep pointing out the good I do. For example, I often say, 'I helped Mother with the dishes!' and 'I am getting A's at school!' It is really hard not to brag a bit, but I am trying."

Haj Abdullah noted, "It would seem you all are ready to move on and continue up those special steps. You are all beautifying your characters, your very beings, by doing what you have learned! So, are you ready to go up the Next Step?"

The children were thrilled! "Yay! Let's go! Let's continue this special journey! Up and away! If not now, when?!"

Imam al-Ghazali

Haj Abdullah agreed, "And do invite some other friends to join in. Let's meet here after your classes tomorrow. I have a surprise story for you."

The Book on the Mysteries of Purity For Children

Finally, throwing up his hands in despair, the scholar shouted impatiently, "Enough! Get out of here, old man!" The old man was promptly shown to the door.

Chapter One
What Is *Wudu*?

The next afternoon the group had grown. Each child had asked several friends whom they thought would be attracted to deeper ideas, and had tried to summarize for them what had been learned from Imam al-Ghazali's Books 1 and 2, the *Book of Knowledge* and the *Book of Belief*.

Beams of afternoon light poured down through the branches of the great tree where they met. A rabbit hopped past. As everyone settled into the special gathering place, Haj Abdullah began. In a solemn tone, he stated: "First, I will tell you a story and please think about what the inner special meaning could be for each one of your precious lives.

"How many of you know how to perform *wudu*, which we perform before our prayers?" All hands went up. "We do! We do!"

Haj Abdullah continued, "Well, maybe you just *think* you do. And perhaps there is *more*!"

The large group of children fell silent. "What could that 'more' be?" they wondered.

The Story

Once upon a time in a little village, there was a grand scholar whom people consulted if they had any questions. Everyone admired him very much for his knowledge!

One day, a very old man leaning on his walking stick, came to the learned man's door and began to knock. The doorkeeper opened the door and this old man began repeating to the scholar

The Book on the Mysteries of Purity For Children

who happened to be standing just inside, "Would you please tell me how to make *wudu*? What *is wudu*?"

The scholar answered in disbelief, "Old man! You have lived in this village your whole life. Of course, you know how to do *wudu*!"

The old man persisted. He kept crying out, "I want to know what is *wudu*? What is *wudu*?!"

Finally, the scholar felt it would be easier to bring this hopeless conversation to an end by simply taking him over to the nearby water tap and performing the steps of *wudu* so that this aged man with his stick could see it. After the scholar completed his demonstration, the old man was asked to duplicate what he had been shown but he got everything wrong! He did the wrong number of washings of the hands. He did everything in the wrong order! Finally, throwing up his hands in despair, the scholar shouted impatiently, "Enough! Get out of here, old man!" The old man was promptly shown to the door.

As the scholar began climbing the stairs to retire to his quarters, he commented to the doorkeeper, "This is very strange! How could an old man of our village, at his age, not know how to perform his ablutions? Why don't you follow him and see what is going on."

After an hour or so the doorkeeper returned and tapped respectfully on the door of the scholar. The moment the scholar opened his door, he noticed with surprise the great concern on the door-keeper's face who explained "Oh, sir, I have to inform you that the old man who couldn't understand what is *wudu* is, in fact, the local holy man, the elder most revered in our village!"

Quietly, the scholar put on his coat and came down the stairs. He then went to present himself at the feet of the beautiful and revered elder. With great humility and downcast eye, he asked very softly, "What is *wudu*?"

Then, the serene and saintly man began to explain very gently. He said, "For example, as you wash your hands, you ask God to forgive you for thoughtless things you may have done and to guide your doings. When you rinse your mouth, you ask God's forgiveness for anything you have said which you have regretted and you pray to God that from this point forward everything that comes from your mouth will be beautiful!

"And when you wash your face, you pray to God that your face may reflect His light in all that you do and may not be darkened by being far from Him. And then, when you cleanse your hands, you ask God's forgiveness for anything you may have done that you now regret and you beg His assistance in helping you do everything in the future which is pleasing to Him. And when you wash your feet, you ask God to forgive you for wherever your feet have taken you that would not be pleasing to Him! And you beg Him to guide you always in the right direction."

And so the proud scholar came to understand that a most important and necessary part of *wudu* is not only an orderly set of outward movements intended to cleanse the body on the outside, but prayers aimed at purifying the inside, polishing the Heart.

"Oh my!" exclaimed Maha, "I had no idea there is so much more we can be doing or thinking when we prepare for our prayers. It sounds like something very important to do."

"And when you think about it, everyone," Yusuf added, "we

are lucky to have *wudu* to do! Imagine, if we just turned from playing to praying with nothing in between!"

"Exactly," continued Khadija, "how odd it would be if I were simply chattering with my friends or watching a film and then suddenly was standing directly before God ﷻ! We really need a way to turn from being busy with things like that to clean or purify these distractions away before we stand before God!"

"Haj Abdullah," Layla asked, "What are the secrets of purity that Imam al-Ghazali tells us about?"

The sun began to set and its golden rays lit up Haj Abdullah's face. The birds were chirping joyously as they settled into the branches of trees for their night's rest. The children moved in closely around their beloved teacher. He spoke softly and they didn't want to miss one word.

Picking up Book Three, their teacher began, "Imam al-Ghazali began his *Book on the Mysteries of Purity* with the words of our blessed Prophet ﷺ.

"Religion is built upon cleanliness," and also, "Purity is the key to prayer." And God Most High says, "Therein are people who love to purify themselves and God loves those who purify themselves" [9:108]. And the Prophet ﷺ also said, "Purification is half of faith," and God Most High says, "God does not want to burden you; He wants to make you pure [5:6]."

Upon hearing these hadiths and Quranic passages, the children felt a wave of awe and seriousness pass over them. Making *wudu* was much more than they had imagined.

"Now children, the Imam wrote about something you all have already begun to understand. He explained that the people with real understanding and knowledge know when our Prophet ﷺ

said, "Purification is half of faith," that what he was saying is that the most important matter is the inward cleaning of your spiritual heart. Wouldn't it be absurd if *wudu* only meant washing parts of your body with water, but leaving your heart dirty and in ruin!"

Abid exclaimed, "Of course! We already know there are two ways of doing things! An outer way and an inner way. Just like there are two kinds of learning! And two kinds of hearts. Both are important."

Abdal Fattah added, "Look at the story of the scholar you just told us. He thought that by doing all the outward motions correctly, he had done a correct *wudu* but then he had to learn from the village's wise man how to be *present* before God while doing it, not just thinking of other things!"

The children all imagined how much fun it would be when each time they washed their hands, they could ask Allah both to forgive any naughty thing they had been doing as well as to guide them in doing something the proper, right way. This would certainly help polish their hearts because making *wudu* several times a day (whenever it was broken) would give them the perfect occasions to remember what is truly important.

Haj Abdullah concluded, "Dear children, try this before you pray. On the day after tomorrow, I will begin to explain the real and deeper meanings that you all want so very much to understand. Over the next days, I will share with you Imam al-Ghazali's precious explanation of certain aspects and mysteries of purification."

Everyone breathed an inward sigh of relief. At last, they would be able to understand what *wudu* is *really* about!

The Book on the Mysteries of Purity For Children

Zainab replied, "For example, while rinsing our mouths, we need to ask God to forgive us for anything we have said that was wrong and ask His help in only saying what pleases Him. The same can be applied to the ears, hands and feet!"

Chapter Two
The Four Levels of Purification:
Cleansing and Purifying Oneself

The neighborhood children arrived in small groups at the sacred garden. Some of the boys climbed up in the trees and pretended to be chirping birds, making everyone laugh.

Haj Abdullah calmly strode in, a peaceful smile on his face. The group assembled around him. He began, "Did you all know there are Four Levels of Purification – four ways that you can be cleansed?"

"Four?" thought Qasim. "That's a lot! I wonder what those could be?"

Haj Abdullah said, "The first way to purify yourself is pretty obvious: you clean yourself from anything that is dirty or impure and that which prevents the prayer. The second way is to purify the various parts of your body from doing wrong or sinful things. I imagine you all have some ideas about this from the story about the scholar, which I told you yesterday. Can anyone give me an example?"

Zainab replied, "For example, while rinsing our mouths, we need to ask God to forgive us for anything we have said that was wrong and ask His help in only saying what pleases Him. The same can be applied to the ears, hands and feet!"

Haj Abdullah smiled with approval and continued, "And the third way to purify yourself is to purify your hearts from low character. Do you remember this from Imam al-Ghazali's *Book of Knowledge*? We have learned of the many things that are wrong to do that dirty our pure, shining Hearts."

The Book on the Mysteries of Purity For Children

Layla picked up from there and went on, "We now understand that we must never argue, be angry or mean, or backbite! Ever! We must want the best for others and be joyful when *they* win a game."

Abid continued, "Right, Layla! We *know* about all these things we should never do – like spying and prying, like hypocrisy or bragging – but we now must *practice* doing them until they become habits – a part of the way we are. Our golden shining hearts must be kept clean!"

Haj Abdullah explained, "What you are all saying is what following the Sunnah or practice of our blessed Prophet ﷺ is about! Just imagine at every single moment of the day that you are acting as he ﷺ would in that situation. Act out of your True Selves, not your false ones."

Then the serene and beautiful elder paused and was silent. The children stopped moving and paid close attention. He then concluded, "Now, the fourth, or highest level of purification would have to do with those steps at the very top of the spiritual stairway, which you read about and illustrated in your workbooks. That is when you are able to purify your soul of *anything* which concerns your lower self. At that stage, even the good deeds, those on the third level, would be like wrongdoings for those on the highest level."

Omar interrupted, "That last fourth level reminds me of the prophets and saints."

"Exactly correct, Omar," Haj Abdullah exclaimed proudly. "But remember, cleansing and purifying are only half of the practice."

"Only *half?*" exclaimed Zainab, quite surprised, yet curious.

"You see, Zainab, the goal you are after is not just cleaning away faults or simply polishing your heart. Why would you clean or polish away all the things that the lower false self wants?"

"Well, could it be that when all the rust or dirty dust is gone, only then can Allah's ﷻ *presence* be fully and completely there?" suggested Qasim. "Could that be the other half? When we have polished our hearts to be like shining mirrors, they will be able to reflect God's Light!"

"Oh, my!" responded Haj Abdullah, "I am so impressed by how much you children have understood! God's Greatness and Majesty cannot be shown to you if your hearts are still full of something else. There is no room for both. As the Quran states, 'And God has not placed two hearts in any person's breast' [33:4]. We have only one spiritual heart."

Yusuf asked, "So if our hearts are polished clean of wrongdoings, then there is room for the virtues, good doings, and following the practices which Islam asks of us. If this hasn't happened, we can't reach the TRUE goal. We have to empty out and then re-fill our hearts."

Fatima added, "It's the same for cleaning the body. Washing is the first of two halves, making it possible for our arms, legs, head, and hands, to be cleansed and *then* filled with acts of worship. You can't pray without washing. That cleaning makes it possible. So it's half of what is needed."

Bilal chimed in, "If you had a glass of dirty water, wouldn't you have to empty it out in order to put clean water in to drink? It's kind of the same idea."

To make the point, one of the children, who had recently joined

The Book on the Mysteries of Purity For Children

the group of special Ghazali friends, put some dirt in his water bottle and all the children exclaimed, "You can't drink that. It won't work anymore as drinking water!"

Haj Abdullah expanded on this good example of the water bottle. "If your body is dirty on the outside as well as on the inside, would you be ready to stand before a great king in that state? Or before Allah ﷻ to pray?"

Everyone sat in silence. None of them liked the idea of feeling dirty on either the inside or the outside of their bodies.

Imam al-Ghazali

The Book on the Mysteries of Purity For Children

Among the special magical features of this garden, which made it a delight for children, was a kind of tree house with many floors. It was made of a series of wooden platforms hidden high up in the branches of the biggest tree. The tree itself was so tall that no one could see its topmost branches. It was a grand and mysterious tree.

Chapter Three
The Magical Tree House and the Levels of Faith

On Friday afternoon, when everyone had returned from the juma'a prayer and had shared in a wonderful family lunch, the neighborhood children gathered in Father Hamza's backyard to play. Among the special magical features of this garden, which made it a delight for children, was a kind of tree house with many floors. It was made of a series of wooden platforms hidden high up in the branches of the biggest tree. The tree itself was so tall that no one could see its topmost branches. It was a grand and mysterious tree. Wooden boards had been nailed up along its trunk like a ladder, making it possible to climb skyward from one platform to another.

Grandfather was sitting in his favorite garden chair sipping mint tea and watching everyone racing around, laughing and playing. Khalid suddenly stopped kicking the ball and bravely admitted to his friends that he found Haj Abdullah's explanation about purification a bit too hard to understand. Grandfather pretended not to be listening, but finally could not resist joining in.

The other children also felt confused and were happy that Grandfather was ready to listen and help. They sometimes felt shy to ask Haj Abdullah too many questions.

The lovely elder put down his tea and reminded them, "Remember when Grandmother and I explained the three selves inside of each of us? That wasn't too hard to understand, was it?"

Everyone nodded in agreement.

Omar thought, "No, it was easy to see how each person has

a lower self that only wants things for itself and has selfish thoughts. And yes, there is another self that is on guard, and corrects the lower self, reminding it to do the higher things that lead it to being its true, real, higher Self, the *Nafs al-Mutma'inna*. But what exactly did this have to do with the levels of purification and what we were told that Imam al- Ghazali called the 'Stations of Faith'? And why had Haj Abdullah told the children that purification was only half of faith? Where *was* the other half? This wasn't at all clear!"

Grandfather pointed to the wooden platforms which rose higher and higher up in the leafy branches of the magnificent and magical tree. "Children, we could call these platforms 'stations' where, like at train or bus stations, one can get on and off and go on to the next. Do you think that you can *ever* reach the very highest one of these platforms, which we can barely see, as it is hidden from sight by shimmering leaves?"

Fatima fearlessly rose to the occasion: "We can only *aim* to reach that higher platform station by reaching the lower ones first. So before we make *wudu*, for example, I guess the first thing we need to do is make sure there are no dirty things on our clothes or bodies like blood, or what comes out when we use the toilet. That's what we do on the first platform, right?

Abdullah jumped up excitedly and added, "I get it now. So on the second platform as we use water to wash certain parts of our bodies, we are also cleaning away the wrong things these parts may have done. Like the mouth that was speaking badly can be filled with praising God instead! And by doing *wudu* correctly we are then able to pray. Prayer is like a doorway to God that's always open! So I see that each of these platforms then is like a station leading on to a next one."

Grandfather smiled and added, "Yes, the four stations of faith are like the four levels of purification. Imagine that there are sets of steps going up to your polished heart. The steps you climb up and over are like the colored dots you all have busily been polishing away, one by one, off the hearts you have drawn. What happens when you clean away something naughty from your character? What comes in its place?"

Qasim replied, "When we empty away something like being greedy and keeping the best for ourselves, then generosity and kindness takes its place. Just like what our teacher Haj Abdullah said. If you clean something away, then, half the process is done. Something better is then able to be in its place – something that is already inside of our Real selves but has gotten covered by dirt!"

Grandfather was delighted. "All right, so that's how you can get up all those steps to reach the third station. That's where you all are busily polishing your hearts removing those things that make a person's character low and ugly. As these are polished away your beautiful good nature and natural virtues shine through brightly."

Everyone gazed up to the third platform. It was high up but was in sight and *could* be reached with continued effort. And they were *already* making this effort every single day!! They were constantly watching and correcting themselves.

Grandfather explained, "That third station way above, that you can barely see, results in your pure Heart. It is still below another very high platform. But that station is the one that is reached by prophets and saintly people who think *only* of God and serve others joyfully. During your lives as you climb up the steps, station by station, the highest platform will become something you understand better and better and you will want to reach. But for now, let's have a closer look at the steps here near the bottom of the tree."

Everyone walked solemnly over to the tree and looked at the first few pieces of wood nailed at its base.

Grandfather questioned, "Who thinks they know what these steps, which lie at the base of the way upward, represent or mean? You can't climb up without them, can you?"

The children thought carefully about this. They knew that the lower self had to be cleansed away and replaced by the true shining self. But they also had learned from Haj Abdullah that there are four levels of cleaning, starting with the body, like doing *wudu*. Zainab exclaimed, "I have an idea! Maybe the first steps at the bottom are learning all *about wudu* and then the first platform is where we get rid of what prevents praying, what is not clean on the outside of both our bodies and clothes."

Qasim added, "And looking for good clean water to wash with. Finding out every detail about this purification! So much to learn and focus on."

"Ah," cautioned Grandfather, "But what could happen if everyone gets so excited about getting their *wudu* so exact and their bodies and clothes so clean that they forget about cleansing their *insides*, their thoughts?"

Ahmed bravely answered Grandfather's question: "If people get too involved in the first level, they might not remember that polishing the Heart is the main goal."

The other children were happy for Ahmed. It was a hard question and most of them were afraid to give a wrong answer in front of the others. They were proud of him.

Grandfather exclaimed, "This is splendid. Well done, Ahmed! Let me tell you all that the first Muslims who lived in the time of the Prophet Muhammad ﷺ and knew him paid a lot of attention to polishing their hearts and didn't over focus on their bodies. But today, I am sad to say, you will meet Muslims who busy themselves excessively, too much, with their clothes and other bodily details and are critical of other people's outward appearance. Shouldn't we all be loving and admiring of another person's inward qualities before all else? We love people who are kind, generous and humble like our blessed Prophet ﷺ. The Prophet ﷺ said that God doesn't look at your bodies or whether you're rich, but rather at your hearts and what you do.

Father Hamza and Mother Haajar had come out into the backyard, having been listening to what Grandfather and the children had been discussing next to the great tree. They joined the conversation.

"Imam al-Ghazali mentioned," added Father, "that there is a group who overly-stresses cleanliness as the base or the foundation of religion and spend most of their time beautifying themselves outwardly, while inside they are in a ruined state, full of pride, conceit, showing off and hypocrisy, all things you children learned about from the Imam's *Book of Knowledge*. In fact, not only did you learn about these harmful vices, you have been making drawings of your own hearts and carefully observing when your lower, false selves are engaged in these low doings. And more than just being aware of these dangers, all of you have been making an effort to polish them away! In the days of the Prophet ﷺ, humble people dressed in poor clothes, which might have been somewhat dirty, and many went barefoot but were pure of heart, focused on inward change. The way these folk looked was described as 'part of faith'. But there are people today who have made things much more difficult than they need to be."

"Oh!" blurted out Omar, "It seems like we don't see many people today who are humble both on the inside and outside – by dressing humbly and working hard on polishing their hearts."

Imam al-Ghazali

God ﷻ wouldn't create us just to watch television and play around. He wants us back with Him and the way to do that is for us to have clean hearts. What fun it is having something REAL to do as we go about our daily lives!"

Chapter Four
Back in the Special Meeting Place

The next day the children excitedly described to Haj Abdullah what Grandfather had tried to explain. Layla talked about the great tree with all the steps leading up to the higher platforms, which seemed too difficult to ever reach!

Haj Abdullah spoke. "If you climb up a hill, it is easy. But to climb to the top of a majestic snow-capped mountain would be very hard. The more precious and noble the goal, the more difficult the way up will be. It will be filled with obstacles, like the rocks that your camels faced on their journey, a story that you will remember from the *Book of Knowledge*. Going up to the higher place can't be done by just wishing for it. In all the fairy tales you may have heard, the hero or heroine faces many trials like dragons and mountains made of ice to be climbed. But imagine that the dragons and trolls are just bad qualities of your *own* lower self that you are trying to polish away! And the mountain of ice, which the heroine somehow must climb, is also inside of us all! The icy mountain is, in a way, like one's heart that is frozen and needs to be melted by your doing good and beautiful warm things. Can anyone think of a way to melt a hard heart?"

"Yes, that is easy," replied Abid, who was ten and had recently joined the group at the last meeting. "We can go up to someone who seems lonely and we can be friendly and warm, not cold. Cold-hearted children leave some children out of games and even tease them."

"And some of my own naughty dragons and trolls," added Fatima, "are not sharing and not being kind which really, I now actually find, are not too hard to correct!"

Little Abdullah continued, "So these difficult places are what we need to climb over, those mountains inside of us. We need to climb over the rocks in the desert journey. We can do it! It's what our lives are for! God ﷻ wouldn't create us just to watch television and play around. He wants us back with Him and the way to do that is for us to have clean hearts. What fun it is having something REAL to do as we go about our daily lives!"

Their Elder added, "Yes, back in the days of the Holy Prophet ﷺ, things were much simpler and people were at ease and not busy criticizing and judging each other all the time. Imam al-Ghazali tells us that their main concern was that their thoughts and hearts were clean and pure. He even tells us that many people at the time of the Prophet ﷺ prayed with their sandals on. Where they lived, they walked on sand and the earth was much cleaner. Once, during a prayer, the Prophet ﷺ removed his sandals because the angel Gabriel let him know that there was something unclean on them. So then when other people began removing their shoes, he ﷺ asked them, 'Why are you taking off your sandals?' A man named al-Nakha'i so disliked the removal of sandals for prayer that he once said, 'I wish some needy person would come and take them all.'"

The children laughed heartily at this!

But then Haj Abdullah explained, "The point Imam al-Ghazali was making by including this story in his third book was that our main concern should not be to think about so many details, but to be present with Allah in our prayers. But can you think of reasons why we do take off our shoes before prayer?"

"Yes," answered Magda. "People might track in dirt from the street and it would be awful putting one's forehead down on

Imam al-Ghazali

the carpet in prayer and then finding a piece of mud."

"That, and even more!" Haj Abdullah went on. "These good and accepted actions, like removing our shoes before prayer, may be ways of coming closer to God, if that is the intention behind them. But the outward acts must not be excessive. We should *never* criticize others who, like the early believers, might not be so exacting."

Zainab added, "Instead of judging others all the time, which we all do, we need to be critical of ourselves!"

Haj Abdullah continued, "That is true, Zainab. So what is the point Imam al-Ghazali is making?"

Bilal jumped in, "I think it is becoming clear to us all. We must focus on polishing our hearts and being noble people and not getting endlessly concerned with tiny outer details, though they have real importance."

"Well said, Bilal," the wise elder stated. "To clean away what is dirty inside like bragging, not sharing and being unkind, is the cleanliness and purity that must be our first concern. Imam al-Ghazali mentions the story of Dawud at-Ta'i. When someone asked him, 'Why don't you take better care of your beard and trim it nicely?' he replied, 'Do you think I have nothing better to do?' What do you think he meant by that reply?"

Maha suggested, "Perhaps what Dawud at-Ta'i was saying was that rather than fiddling around worrying about perfecting his beard so much, he was busy with his prayers and helping others."

"Exactly, Maha," Haj Abdullah continued. "The early Believers avoided what was not clean or impure, but they did not look into minute and tiny possibilities. Instead, they were extremely careful not to show off or be unfair in any way! Instead of worrying about all the outer things, which might not be pure, they really concerned themselves with the inner ones. If we are not working on our lower self, that cunning false self will take over."

Layla, who had been quiet for a very long time, finally spoke up. It was clear she had listened carefully. "So what we must do, dear Haj Abdullah, is to be *sure* to do what is the most important and pay attention to the details of how to use our lives doing what is best, instead of just wanting more and more things in this world!"

As the moon came out, everyone sat silently. To be created a human being! What a great gift from Allah ﷻ and what a shame it would be to waste it.

Imam al-Ghazali

With all this talk of keeping clean, little Ibrahim inquired earnestly, "But we get dirty when we play outside!" To which Haj Abdullah replied, "There are a few things you needn't worry about, like the dirt which gets on your clothes...What you are learning here is that our Revealed Law excuses certain kinds of impurity or dirtiness, and that ritual purity is based on ease and not hardship."

Chapter Five
Some Parts of Outward Purity

The children were definitely ready to begin learning the necessary details about cleanliness and purity. They loved the orderly way in which Imam al-Ghazali explained everything. They were grateful to their families and Haj Abdullah for selecting out the parts from the Imam's books which he wrote for grown-ups but which would be useful for them during childhood.

The ever-increasing group of children had gathered on a weekend morning and eagerly awaited their teacher. They were playing "Hide and Go Seek" when he appeared, looking radiant as always. The children gathered around and took their places under the great tree which was their own very special meeting place.

Haj Abdullah inquired, "Children, do you think that there is anything which is not alive – the things we call "inanimate" – that is impure or not clean?"

Yusuf thought about this and wondered, "How about the rocks in our garden or the dust on tables and chairs?"

"Believe it or not, children," the Elder replied, "we believe that all non-living things are pure and clean except for wine and other drinks that can make people drunk, which would be such a sad state for people to be in. And what about living, animate, or moving creatures?"

Maryam contributed, "We have all been raised to know that dogs and pigs are not clean, even though dogs help and protect us, but is there anything more?"

The Book on the Mysteries of Purity For Children

"Yes, Maryam. Dead creatures are ritually unclean except for five: dead human beings, fish, locusts, apple worms and bugs. Insects have no blood, like flies and beetles. If these insects fall into water which you might want to use for your *wudu*, the water is still pure to use."

Khalid asked, "What do you mean by *ritually* unclean?"

"Ah, of course!" Haj Abdullah went on to explain. "Acts of worship which we do for God ﷻ are called 'rites,' like the ritual of prayer, or the ritual of fasting or pilgrimage. So, for offering our ritual prayers, which God ﷻ has asked of us, we must be 'ritually' clean, a *special* kind of purity. When you play football, you do not need to be ritually clean because such a game is not an act of worship like prayer."

Khalid was confused. "Did you mean 'rights' like right and wrong? I didn't know 'rights' had anything to do with rituals."

Haj Abdullah explained, "No, Khalid, these two words sound the same, but I was talking about 'rites' – spelled differently than 'rights.' Rites are certain actions we do for God. For us, the first of these rites is the Prayer."

He continued with the lesson: "So there are some wet substances which come from our body which are pure and some which are not."

Bilal understood. "Yes, our parents taught us that. What comes out of us when we go to the bathroom."

Haj Abdullah nodded. "Yes, so those are two things, and there is one more: blood. If we have that on our clothes, on our hands, or on the prayer rug, we have to wash it off. But what about tears? Are they pure or not? What do you think?"

The children thought a minute, but then Ismael said, "I think they are pure."

Their teacher said, "That's right, and the same is true for perspiration which comes out of our bodies when we are hot, or saliva, the wetness in our mouths and mucous – what we sometimes get in our noses. What's the difference between these and the substances that are not pure?"

Ismael offered, "Well, I heard that perspiration, sweating is good for us because it cools our skin, so is it anything our bodies make that is good for us?"

Haj Abdullah nodded again. "Our bodies make tears, sweat, saliva, and mucous when we need them and they help us."

With all this talk of keeping clean, little Ibrahim inquired earnestly, "But we get dirty when we play outside!" to which Haj Abdullah replied, "There are a few things you needn't worry about, like the dirt which gets on your clothes. If your clothes get dirty, naturally they are washed. Also, don't worry about what is still stuck on your shoes' soles after you brush off anything you can. And no worry about the little bit of blood you may get on your clothes if you get scratched or swat a tiny mosquito. What you are learning here is that our Revealed Law excuses certain kinds of impurity or dirtiness, and that ritual purity is based on *ease* and not hardship."

The children were learning new ideas and were now curious about water itself.

The Book on the Mysteries of Purity For Children

Haj Abdullah replied, "Water in itself is clean and pure, but if there is something in it or it's touching something that changes its color, or how it tastes or smells, then we can't use it for the wudu. This is what our Prophet ﷺ taught us when he said, "Water was created pure and nothing makes it impure except what changes its color, taste or smell."

Chapter Six
Washing With Water

Adam asked, "Can we make our *wudu* in just any water? We swim in the pond near our home but the water looks brown and kind of smells."

Haj Abdullah replied, "Water in itself is clean and pure, but if there is something in it or it's touching something that changes its color, or how it tastes or smells, then we can't use it for the *wudu*. This is what our Prophet ﷺ taught us when he said, "Water was created pure and nothing makes it impure except what changes its color, taste or smell."

Amina wondered, "What if we had a big jug of water and some milk or vinegar fell in? Could we still use it for *wudu*?"

The wise elder pointed out that it is in the nature of water and other liquids to change anything small that falls into them, into themselves. The larger amount overwhelms the smaller amount. If you threw a cup of chicken broth into a large pool of water, the soup would vanish and become part of the pool's water.

"And," suggested Fatima, "If you added a cup of water to a large pot of chicken broth, you wouldn't be able to find the cup of water, would you? And what if we washed my doll's dress in a big bucket of water or my Kitty had a drink from this water, it would still be pure for me to use in my ablutions, wouldn't it?"

"That's right, Fatima, and especially about your kitty. Do you know that some of the companions of our Prophet ﷺ made sure that water pots were not covered up so that if a cat were thirsty, she could drink from them? And that was the same water they used for *wudu*."

Fatima thought that was a kind thing to do and decided to make sure that she remembered to give her kitty fresh water in her bowl.

Ibrahim called out, "Everyone! Next time we are here playing in this garden and it is time for prayer, I know what we can do! There is no water faucet but there is a stream coming from the mountains. We can see if the water has a good smell, taste or color!"

Imam al-Ghazali

"I carry one with me," added Haj Abdullah. *"It is an easy way to clean my teeth and freshen my mouth wherever I am. He held up a small stick whose tip end had been cut and looked like bristles. The Messenger of God ﷺ said, 'Verily your mouths are pathways of the Quran, so sweeten them with the toothstick.' Now, when we pray, don't we recite passages from the Quran and mention God ﷻ Most High?" The children nodded solemnly. This was indeed true.*

Chapter Seven
The Toothbrush

The very next afternoon, the neighborhood children hurried to the special garden. Everyone was curious about what their wise teacher might tell them about the mysteries and *meanings* of doing *wudu* itself. This sounded promising and exciting.

The children were surprised when Haj Abdullah opened the meeting by asking, "What do you suppose people used to brush their teeth with before the very recent invention of modern toothbrushes made from different colored plastic?"

Isa answered, "I went with my parents on Hajj and I saw people from every place on earth. Many carried small toothsticks that stuck out of their pockets. They looked like tiny branches cut from a tree. My father said these are called *siwak*. We bought some in Medina and we enjoy using them at home. The taste is very fresh."

"I carry one with me," added Haj Abdullah. "It is an easy way to clean my teeth and freshen my mouth wherever I am. He held up a small stick whose tip end had been cut and looked like bristles. The Messenger of God ﷺ said, 'Verily your mouths are pathways of the Quran, so sweeten them with the toothstick.' Now, when we pray, don't we recite passages from the Quran and mention God ﷻ Most High?" The children nodded solemnly. This was indeed true.

"And he ﷺ also said, 'The prayer offered after having used the toothstick is better than 75 prayers without having used it.'"

The children could see it coming. There would be a lot more brushing of teeth in the future. But anyway, they always felt

The Book on the Mysteries of Purity For Children

so much cleaner and fresher after brushing their teeth.

Abid was curious. "But I don't think we have those sticks here in our town. I have never seen one before. What should we do?"

Their teacher answered, "What's important is that we have some kind of toothbrush and that we use it regularly – our Prophet ﷺ brushed his teeth so often that his Companions thought it might become a law! If you are going to use a toothbrush especially before *wudu*, however, you must brush your teeth without toothpaste. Before you go to bed, of course, and any time you brush your teeth besides for *wudu*, you can use toothpaste."

Haj Abdullah concluded the discussion about the tooth stick saying, "The Prophet ﷺ said that he didn't want to make things difficult for his community. Otherwise, he would have asked that the toothstick be used before every single prayer."

Zainab exclaimed, "That's not too hard. I will try to brush my teeth before each of my prayers." The other children thought Zainab was good to speak up, but were not sure they wanted to carry a toothbrush around with them all day long. It would probably get lost and their mothers would complain.

The dear elder added, "Let us just say that it would be better, *preferred,* to brush your teeth for every prayer and at the start of every ablution, or *wudu*, you make. It is also thoughtful to clean your breath if you eat something with a strong smell that might be unpleasant for others and also it is good to brush whenever you awake from sleep. Also, if you can, don't just brush across your teeth, but up and down as well. Let us now turn to the mysteries of *wudu* itself."

Imam al-Ghazali

So, of course, when we rinse our mouth it is good to ask Allah ﷻ to help us when we recite the Holy Quran, His very words! And, also I will be asking Him to help me only say beautiful, helpful things, every day, and maybe to be a bit more quiet."

Chapter Eight
How to Begin *Wudu*: The Mouth

"Who knows what we say before we begin anything?" asked the wise teacher.

The children cried out in unison, "'In the Name of God, the All-Merciful, and Compassionate.' We say this a lot every day. So, of course, we say this when we begin our *wudu*."

Haj Abdullah added, "Imam al-Ghazali mentions that the Prophet ﷺ said that if we don't mention God's name ﷻ, our *wudu* is not even complete and that we should also ask God's ﷻ protection from the low suggestions of devils, before washing."

Abid added, "What that means, everyone, is that we must be on our guard for low thoughts and ideas which might come into our minds! It is very good that we already have been learning how to watch out for just this kind of thing!" Everyone nodded in agreement.

"And children," their wise teacher further explained, "after washing your hands three times, don't forget that for your *wudu* to be acceptable you must make the intention that you are doing it to remove impurities or to be able to pray. You need to keep this intention in your mind even up through washing your face.

"Next, take three handfuls of water with your right hand and rinse out your mouth three times. Here is what Imam al-Ghazali suggests that you say: 'O God, help me in the recitation of your Book and to remember You abundantly.'"

Layla piped up, "We understand from the story about the

The Book on the Mysteries of Purity For Children

scholar and the village wise man that there certainly are a lot of really important things we could all be thinking and praying about during *wudu*. So, of course, when we rinse our mouth, it is good to ask Allah ﷻ to help us when we recite the Holy Quran, His very words! And, also I will be asking Him to help me only say beautiful, helpful things, every day, and maybe to be a bit more quiet."

Some of the children giggled because it did seem that Layla talked an awful lot. But mainly they were impressed with her decisions. They, too, would be thinking of ways to improve their speech and maybe even the kinds of food they took into their mouths.

Haj Abdullah was pleased that the children were joining in with thoughtful ways in which they could continue polishing their hearts, even during *wudu*.

Imam al-Ghazali

The Book on the Mysteries of Purity For Children

I can just imagine the Garden of Paradise with all the scented flowers. Breathing in drops of the clean water seems to be a kind of way of connecting to it."

Chapter Nine
The Nose

"So, what does Imam al-Ghazali say we should ask for when we rinse our noses?" inquired Yusef.

Haj Abdullah answered, "As we sniff, or breathe in the refreshing water three times we could pray 'Oh God ﷻ, let me smell the perfume of Heaven and may You be pleased with me.'"

Bilal exclaimed. "I like that idea very much. I think about the Next Heavenly World a lot, where now some of my relatives are. I can just imagine the Garden of Paradise with all the scented flowers. Breathing in drops of the clean water seems to be a kind of way of connecting to it."

"And when we blow out the water that we sniffed in, that is like pushing us away or removing us far from the dark smelly place where the really bad people might end up for a while after they die. Yes, and Imam al-Ghazali tells us that when we blow out, we need to ask God ﷻ to protect us from that dark place," said Abid.

The Book on the Mysteries of Purity For Children

"Yes, the face is very, very important. It's what we first notice about one another. Imam al-Ghazali said that an excellent prayer when cleansing the face is 'O God, brighten my face with Your Light on the Day when the Face of Your friends are brightened, and do not darken my face with Your darkness on the Day when some people's faces will be dark."

Chapter Ten
The Brightened Face

"What does Imam al-Ghazali tell us about the rinsing of the face?" asked their wise teacher.

Every hand eagerly went up. Sara blurted out, "We take handfuls of water three times and go from the top of the forehead down to our chins, going as wide as to our ears! I love the feeling of the water dashed over my eyebrows and eyelashes. I feel so bright afterwards."

"And," added Yacoub, "Don't forget about the eye sockets. You can use your index fingers-just like this!"

As the boy demonstrated, the children all began to speak at once. "We can easily guess what we should pray for while we wipe around our eyes!"

"That we not look at awful things!"

"That we not spy on or envy what we see!"

"That we look for the beautiful qualities in others!"

"Wonderful, Children!" exclaimed their teacher, so proud that they could come up with such good ideas which could be used as they washed their faces. He concluded, "Yes, the face is very, very important. It's what we first notice about one another. Imam al-Ghazali said that an excellent prayer when cleansing the face is 'O God, brighten my face with Your Light on the Day when the Face of Your friends are brightened, and do not darken my face with Your darkness on the Day when some people's faces will be dark."

The young people whispered this prayer amongst themselves.

The Book on the Mysteries of Purity For Children

They were certainly aiming to be God's friends. By polishing their hearts, day by day, they could feel that their faces were more and more shining and bright! They would think of this when they rinsed their faces.

Imam al-Ghazali

The Book on the Mysteries of Purity For Children

"The Prophet ﷺ said, 'Whoever is able, let him extend the places washed,' and 'A splendorous Light will reach whatever places the ablution reached.'"

Chapter Eleven
Shining Hands and Forearms

Haj Abdullah explained that just as their purified faces would be shining in the Next World, when the faithful gathered on the Day of Resurrection, so too would any parts of their bodies shine which were rinsed in their *wudu*. "The Prophet ﷺ said, 'Whoever is able, let him extend the places washed,' and 'A splendorous Light will reach whatever places the ablution reached.'"

Little Abdullah contributed, "Well, then, when I wash my feet, I will extend the water way up above my ankles! The more Light the better!"

"Exactly," praised their wise mentor. "Exactly! And as you wash your right hand three times you could ask Allah ﷻ that on the Day when you are presented with the book listing what you did before you died, He will give it to you in your right hand and be easy on you. Just as when you wash your left hand three times, you might seek God's protection from receiving your book in your left hand or behind your back" (Quran 17:71; 69:19; 84:07; 69:25; 84:10).

The children were all thinking of both the good things which they could do with their hands, as well as other not-so-good things which they would try to avoid.

The Book on the Mysteries of Purity For Children

The beautiful sounds in nature like the singing of birds or the waves breaking on the shore reminded them of heaven.

Chapter Twelve
The Top of The Head and The Neck

Sara was selected to demonstrate the next step. She wet her hands and joined the fingertips of both hands and then, starting from the hair just above her forehead, she wiped the top of her head running all the way down to the neck. She didn't forget to then separate her hands and bring them back along each side of the neck to the front. Everyone copied her for the three times and then looked up at their wise elder to hear what Imam al-Ghazali recommended as an accompanying prayer. He had written this on a piece of paper. Everyone leaned in upon one another so that they could read together: 'O Allah, cover me with Your Mercy, send down upon me Your blessings and shade me in the shade of Your Throne on the Day when there is no shade except Your shade.'

Silence fell over the group. These were very beautiful words. Indeed, all people want God's Mercy and Blessings every moment of their lives. This would be a very good thing to ask God ﷻ as they wiped over their heads. And by passing their hands over their heads they would be reminded of the shade of God's Throne in the world to come. Each child imagined this awesome moment. They all definitely wanted to be in the shade of God's throne.

Abid then offered to show how the ears were wiped. He asked that everyone place their wet index finger gently into each ear hole. The children tried not to giggle because it really was amusing seeing everyone do this at the same time. Then Abid asked them to place their thumbs up behind the tops of their ears and wipe down in an arching shape like a 'C'. After that, they were to cover both entire ears and wipe over them lightly

The Book on the Mysteries of Purity For Children

– all of course for three times. The children could guess what the suitable prayer might be like. Each young person was thinking of what kinds of things one should and shouldn't listen to. The beautiful sounds in nature like the singing of birds or the waves breaking on the shore reminded them of heaven. Maha thought to herself, "I should listen to my Mother when she is kindly advising me." Daud counseled himself, "Don't listen to the boys when they invite me to throw rocks at birds."

Haj Abdullah interrupted their musings. "O God ﷻ. Ya Allah, make me among those who hear what is said and follow the best of it. God, let me hear the one who will call to Heaven and for me to be righteous." Quran (39:18). Lastly, the neck is wiped only once with fresh water, from back to front.

Imam al-Ghazali

The Book on the Mysteries of Purity For Children

"But aren't there special prayers we could be saying as we rinse our feet?" inquired Maha. "I can think of lots of things I am going to say, like, 'Dear God, please take my feet in a direction of doing things that make You happy with me, such as into the kitchen to help Mother.

Chapter Thirteen
Finally, Your Feet

"Could someone please draw a pair of bare feet on a sheet of paper?" suggested Haj Abdullah. "You will see why this is helpful."

Sara was artistic and leapt at the chance to draw anything, even if it were just outlines of feet.

Haj Abdullah pointed to the fine illustration and reminded the children that a person always begins with the right first. As one begins by washing the right foot three times, one must wash between each of the toes, using the left hand.

"Now look at the drawing everyone. Do you see the little toe on the right foot? This is where you begin washing between your toes, then you begin moving over to the space next to the big toe."

Abid asked, "Do we do the same thing when we wash the left foot three times?"

"Good question, Abid. Actually, the reason Sara's drawing is useful is because you can see that instead of beginning with the little toe of your left foot, you instead start with the big toe."

Sara commented, "Kind of like going up a hill starting on the far right and then when we reach the top where the two big toes are, we go down from there to the little toe on the far left. If any of you are confused, draw your own drawing and number the toes 1 to 10."

Little Abdullah got a stick and outlined his two feet in the earth. Then he put numbers above each toe and added, "Now,

The Book on the Mysteries of Purity For Children

I get it!"

"But aren't there special prayers we could be saying as we rinse our feet?" inquired Maha. "I can think of lots of things I am going to say, like, 'Dear God, please take my feet in a direction of doing things that make You happy with me, such as into the kitchen to help Mother instead of to some place where I'll just watch TV or play a game on the computer. I mean, everyone, here are more *great* ways to polish our hearts!"

"Maha is right," exclaimed Yusuf. "Look at how many ideas for polishing our hearts come from washing each part of our body during *wudu*! It's amazing, really."

Haj Abdullah beamed with contentment to see how these young people understood that *wudu* is not only outer movements and cleaning, but is an inner cleansing and an aid to remind us about being pure inside.

Bilal raised his hand, "Isn't it better to wash all the way up our calves if we can?"

"Good for you, Bilal, for remembering! Yes, we must wash all the way to our ankles and it's good if we can wash a bit further up our legs, too!"

And once your *wudu* is complete, you repeat the shahada – and sometimes the Prophet ﷺ would look up towards the sky when he did this. Then, admit you have done some things you are not proud of and say, 'Oh God ﷻ, I turn to You in repentance so forgive me and accept my repentance. You truly are the Forgiving and the Compassionate! Oh God, Make me among those who turn to You in repentance and make me among those who purify themselves and make me among Your righteous servants and make me Your patient and grateful servant, among those who invoke You much and glorify You early and late.' Imam al-Ghazali tells us that if you make this prayer at the end of your *wudu*, it will rise up for you to beneath Allah's Throne where it will continue to glorify Him and will also be there among your good deeds waiting for you after your death. But if you can't remember all that, just say the shahada."

This was an awful lot for the children to take in, but it showed how important it is to say these special prayers while making *wudu*.

Zainab exclaimed, "Maybe our parents can say that prayer. It's long. But we can certainly say it in an easier way. We do know the shahada already. We can all ask God to forgive us and help us to be more patient, grateful and correct in our doings and to remember Him when we wake up in the morning and go to sleep at night. I can do that!"

The other children were relieved that Zainab had spoken and they all breathed an inner sigh of relief.

The crescent moon appeared and gleamed through the branches of the trees, which hung over and protected the special, sacred, meeting place. Everyone sat in peaceful silence thinking about this new and important teaching. It would certainly be more enriching to do *wudu* NOW that they could understand the *inner* meanings.

"What would it be like if you invited a great king to your house and, to prepare for his visit, you very carefully polished the outside of the door while the inside of the house was a mess and full of rubbish? What would the king think? It is the same as if God ﷻ watched us making our wudu. And one of His Ninety-Nine Names is al-Malik, the King."

Chapter Fourteen
More Helpful Information

That night, Bilal decided to try out what he had learned. It seemed like a lot to remember but he was excited to try. His father walked past the open bathroom door and could see a special effort was being made. Usually, the children just rushed through their ablutions. Parents, of course, are very knowledgeable about the practices of Islam and, over time, explain these carefully according to the ages of their sons and daughters.

When Bilal finished, Father Hamza praised him and commented, "I see you are making wonderful and thoughtful efforts with your *wudu*. Now that you are more grown-up, would you like me to give you a few extra pointers?

"First, be careful not to do more than three washings. People sometimes forget how many washings they have done, but our Prophet ﷺ also warned us against wasting water and over focusing on *wudu*.

"Second, because we must all be careful not to waste water, we should not *splash* it on our faces.

"And something else. Every so often, someone comes and speaks to us while we are doing our *wudu*. But talking during *wudu* is usually not acceptable; it's all right to answer someone if they say '*as-salamu 'alaykum*,' but it's better if we concentrate on what we're doing."

Bilal was very grateful for this guidance. He wanted to share some of what he had been learning.

"Dad, I have been learning that *wudu* happens in two places.

The Book on the Mysteries of Purity For Children

People can see us washing on the outside but Allah ﷻ looks at how our hearts are being cleaned and made pure on the inside."

Father Hamza was delighted to hear this. "My dear son! I am so happy to hear what you are saying – and doing! I have been watching you and your friends really making progress with your hearts, noticing problems, and polishing away vices and letting all your natural virtues shine through."

Mother Haajar, who had joined in, then told a useful Ghazali story. "What would it be like if you invited a great king to your house and, to prepare for his visit, you very carefully polished the outside of the door while the inside of the house was a mess and full of rubbish? What would the king think? It is the same as if God ﷻ watched us making our *wudu*. And one of His Ninety-Nine Names is al-Malik, the King."

Bilal thought this would be a good story to tell the others. Maybe everyone, or at least Sara, could draw this house or a person, with the lovely outside and the inside full of trash. A very good reminder indeed!

Imam al-Ghazali

The Book on the Mysteries of Purity For Children

The Prophet ﷺ said, "There is no Muslim who goes to sleep in a state of purity, remembering God, then arises from the night and asks for the goodness in this world and the next except that God gives that to him."

Chapter Fifteen
Breakfast at Grandmother's

On the weekend when there was no school, Zainab, Layla, Abdullah and Bilal often had a really yummy breakfast cooked by their Grandmother. She did eggs in a special way simmered in tomato cooked in olive oil. Everyone dipped pieces of bread into a central plate and enjoyed delicious bites of this tasty treat.

Grandmother was having her morning coffee, which she enjoyed very much.

"Children, I hear from the family that now you are all learning to do *wudu* in the best way possible. Can I tell you about something very special I read in Imam al-Ghazali's *Book on the Mysteries of Purification*?"

The children were not sure they wanted to hear about this at breakfast, but there was no stopping Grandmother Aisha when she had something she longed to share. They went on eating but looked up with respect and even interest.

"The Messenger of God ﷺ said that if we can perform the *wudu* very well and then afterwards pray a prayer of two bowings, *concentrating* on what we are doing and not thinking about every other thought that comes into our minds, we will finish that prayer and be as pure as the day our mothers gave birth to us and God will forgive us for every wrong thing we have ever done."

Abdullah thought to himself, "There never seems to be an end to what we can do to make our *wudu* even better! But on the other hand, if two *rakahs* of prayer could make one as pure

The Book on the Mysteries of Purity For Children

as the day one was born – well – that was *really* great and definitely a good thing to do whenever possible."

Grandmother, of course, continued, "Yes, our blessed Prophet ﷺ told us many important things about our ablutions, our *wudu*. Did you know that we are lifted up and made purer if we do our *wudu* carefully and perfectly when the conditions are extremely difficult? For example, if you are out playing far from a water tap, you might just need to use some collected rainwater. Or maybe you are in a place that is freezing cold and wetting your feet will be hard, indeed. But we know that God does not accept your prayers without this washing. He loves this *wudu* very much!"

The children imagined what it would be like making *wudu* in the snow. God would really be pleased!

Grandmother knew many *hadith* by heart which impressed the children a lot. She continued to explain to them that even if they had not broken their state of *wudu* but renewed it anyway, the Prophet ﷺ said that this was like *Light upon Light* and God would also record for them ten extra good deeds.

"Children! *Do* try very, very hard to remember God while you are doing your *wudu*. If you do this, He will purify your *entire* bodies – not just the places where the water touched."

Zainab put down her fork and stated, "Grandmother, we may seem to be busy eating breakfast but what we hear Imam al-Ghazali saying really shows us, more and more, what a huge opportunity we are being given. What a gift! All these many, many ways to be pure and to polish our hearts!"

"And," Grandmother went on, "Imam al-Ghazali reminds us that when we rinse our mouths, the bad things we've said to other people leave from our mouths. And when we wash our faces and ears and hands and feet, any bad things we've seen or heard or done with them depart us– leaving us even from under our eyelids and from under our fingernails and toenails!"

Layla imagined drawing an outline of a person with their bad deeds leaving, coming out like rays from all these places. Yes, she would draw this. It would help remind her of all the many ways not-nice doings could leave. She said, "Grandmother, we have a friend who has told us a story about a wise man and scholar that reminds me of this hadith which you just told us. As we wash each part, we can say we are sorry and ask forgiveness for what that body part shouldn't have done and to pray for it to change its ways. Like our ears shouldn't listen to bad things but only good."

Grandmother wondered who this knowledgeable friend might be. The children had not yet told her about Haj Abdullah.

Zainab added, "And, our special teacher recommended that after we do our *wudu*, carefully, we should say the shahada."

"What a fine teacher you have," added Grandmother. "Did he tell you that Imam al-Ghazali mentions that if you say the shahada after *wudu*, the eight gates of Heaven are opened to you and you can enter through *any* one you wish."

Sara began drawing a Paradisal Garden with eight entrance gates on a paper napkin. Grandmother sipped her coffee and sighed happily. "Something you could say before you go to sleep is: 'Whatever gifts I or anyone else have are from You, so I thank You and give praise to You.'"

Imam al-Ghazali reminds us that if you get in bed at night and are pure, having just made your *wudu*, and then you remember

The Book on the Mysteries of Purity For Children

Allah ﷻ and ask His forgiveness, it is an excellent thing to do. Why? Because imagine if you died while asleep. God will take us back to Him in the condition He finds us at the moment of death He has chosen for us. But then, if we awake and didn't die, we can ask Allah ﷻ for goodness in this world and the Next world as well – and God will give this to us!"

The children were stunned by all this talk of dying in their sleep. Grandmother was old so she was interested in that kind of thing, but on the other hand they *did* know of children who had died, some even in their sleep. As they pushed back their chairs from the breakfast table and went out to play with their friends, Yusuf commented, "Maybe it's not too hard to go to bed pure, just in case!"

Imam al-Ghazali

The Book on the Mysteries of Purity For Children

When we see a rainbow in the sky, a beautiful sunset, and the shimmering moon above a majestic mountain, we are reminded of God's ﷻ amazing creation of this world and the Next. If we see something beautiful, it can help us recall what our true goal is.

Chapter Sixteen
In What Way Should We Try to Look Beautiful?

The neighborhood children were taught much about their religion and its practices at home by their parents.

Mother Haajar had loved reading the grown-ups' book of Imam al-Ghazali's *Book on the Mysteries of Purity*, and as her children grew up, she gradually shared with them what would be useful for them to learn at different ages, or when a situation took place for which Imam al-Ghazali's teachings would be a help.

One of the things which everyone loved in the *Book of Knowledge* was the idea that we are all teachers, whether young or old. The children certainly noticed that they copied the friends they liked and admired. And Imam al-Ghazali had made it clear that we would never want to do or *be* something we would not like others to copy.

Zainab was dressing for school and had chosen some casual clothes that Mother Haajar thought would be better only worn at home. Even though this outfit was not very dignified, or even pretty, Zainab explained, "Mother, I really want to wear this because this is what the other girls wear to school."

Mother understood but answered, "Zainab, one of your special qualities is that you are a teacher of what is good. If you dress like that, your friends will not take some of the fine things you have to say seriously. What would you think if your Quran teacher wore jeans? When people dress in a beautiful and noble way, others respect what they say. We would not wish to turn others away from the good that we have to offer simply because the way we look is not dignified, would we?"

The Book on the Mysteries of Purity For Children

"It is true, Mother, that God ﷻ loves us to meet others looking beautiful, while not trying to impress them or attract a lot of attention. I even know, inside, that the reason I want to dress like the others is to show off some of my clothes, just because I want them to like me. But I guess if my friends just liked me because of my clothes, rather than because I had a good heart, they wouldn't really be the kind of friends I would want to have!"

"Good for you!" replied Zainab's mother. "You don't need to show off things, but you do need to teach others by dressing with the kind of dignity that fits with your good character. That is, be the kind of person you would like copied. I am sure this is your true golden heart rather than fancy clothes and bracelets. We all want to be beautiful but, in the truest way."

Her mother continued, "Imam al-Ghazali also tells us that seeing something that is really beautiful reminds us of Heaven! And so someone dressing or acting in a beautiful way reminds us of the Next World which lasts forever. Seeing ugly things warns us to watch out for what is bad in our lives.

Zainab agreed. "If we see something beautiful, it can help us recall what our true goal is. If I do something and my real intention is just to show off, I should really notice that I am not being my True Real Self. We learned all that from Grandmother, about the three selves. So all day long, when I notice myself being lazy, or selfish or greedy, these are reminders that I should be polishing my Heart which is all that can come with me to Heaven."

Mother Haajar hugged Zainab. "Isn't it wonderful that absolutely everything, *every* moment can help us to be who we really and truly are! And help us make sense and understand the meaning of what we are supposed to be doing in this life! When we see a rainbow in the sky, a beautiful sunset, and the shimmering moon above a majestic mountain, we are reminded of God's ﷻ amazing creation of this world and the *Next*."

Zainab ran outside and looked up into a tree. She noticed a mother bird feeding her baby. The baby kept dropping the worm but the mother bird patiently picked it up and fed it to the baby. Zainab thought to herself, "I can copy that mother bird and be more patient with everyone!"

The Book on the Mysteries of Purity For Children

"A beautiful light will reach the places the ablutions reached."
Muslim 250

Chapter Seventeen
The Order in Which We Do Things

Bilal and Abdullah had been in the backyard digging in the earth. They were building a fort out of mud and it was a lot of fun. When Mother called them in for supper, they at first were thinking they would pretend not to hear her. They were happy digging. But these days, now that Haj Abdullah had been advising the children, they really wanted to polish their hearts. The last thing they needed was to add colored dots on their heart drawings, for being dishonest and unkind to mother.

They shook off the excess dirt from their clothes and kicked their shoes against a tree, to dislodge mud. Coming in through the kitchen door, they washed their hands in the sink. Father Hamza had come in to carry out the large soup bowl to the table when he noticed their hands. He noticed a lot of dirt under his sons' fingernails and commented, "After supper I will show you how to trim your nails. They are a bit long and so are hard to keep clean. I am sure this lesson would add some useful bits to your whole program for studying and practicing *wudu* and purity."

After dinner, Father and sons retreated to the bathroom. Their father began, "Imam al-Ghazali wrote that although both fingernails and toenails must be trimmed, the hand is more noble than the foot and therefore should come first. And as the right hand is more noble that the left, one should begin there. But let me ask you boys: of your five fingers on your right hand, which do you think is sort of like the leader of the rest, or the best finger?" They both held up their index fingers.

"That's right! And why did you choose that one?"

The Book on the Mysteries of Purity For Children

The boys answered, "Because it's the finger we raise when we say the shahada after the ablution and when we are doing our prayers."

"That's exactly right" Father Hamza said.

"I have learned that the Prophet ﷺ trimmed his fingernails beginning with his right index finger and then finished with his right thumb before moving on to his left hand. But I'm going to show you how Imam al-Ghazali teaches us to do it."

Father got out the small fingernail scissors. Showing the boys the right order was much easier than simply talking about it.

So after trimming Bilal's index finger first and then moving to the right, Father reached his son's right hand's little finger. But then Father Hamza put both his palms and all of his fingertips together. He pointed out that a kind of circle was made. Abdullah and Bilal tried this out. So instead of going back to the right thumb, which the boys expected, he went from the little finger of the right hand to the little finger of the left and then around to the thumb of the left hand ending with the thumbnail of the right.

This was something! The boys would need to draw this and demonstrate the process to all their friends. They imagined it would make Haj Abdullah smile.

But the lesson was not over! Their dad asked them to take off their shoes and socks. Even though their feet had not had direct contact with the dirt around their feet, their toes and toenails were pretty dirty to behold. There were lots of dark bits under the nails, which were very much in need of trimming. The boys felt slightly embarrassed by all the dirt under their nails. However, their father pointed out that it is really quite easy to wash away these small amounts of dirt on the outer body as compared to the countless dirty vices to be polished away from the inside. Rinsing away the outer dirt was a *good reminder* that there is plenty of inner dirt that is more harmful.

"Boys," continued Father, "you are certainly old enough to regularly trim your own nails. Here are scissors for each of you. Put your right feet up on the edge of the tub and begin with your big right toes. Imam al-Ghazali points out that as there is no toe which is equal to the importance of the index finger (which you hold up as you say the shahada), the feet form a single row when placed firmly together on the ground."

Bilal and Abdullah placed their bare feet on the floor together. Abdullah thought another helpful drawing would be of use to convey this next trimming order for the feet to the group in the sacred garden.

Abdullah began clipping his big right toe nail and then moved out to his right little toe, not quite sure what to do next, anymore! Bilal followed along cautiously. Father knew trouble lay ahead and advised, "Now that you both have completed your right foot, move *all* the way left and start with the little toenail of the left foot."

They reached the left big toe and noticed with relief how clean and tidy their feet now looked.

Abdullah could not resist asking his father about a major concern and worry he had since all these many lessons on *wudu* and purity had come into their lives.

Bravely, he asked, "Father, all we ever hear about anymore is 'Do three of these, then do this, after that!' So many numbers in everything we have to do. The order of the bowings and everything else in our prayer seems pretty easy compared to all this information concerning being clean and *wudu*. I am pretty confused, to be honest."

Bilal was happy that Abdullah had been the one to express these worries. He felt too shy.

"Oh, of course!" exclaimed Father Hamza. "I have been so busy with all the practical details that I nearly forgot to explain. Imam al-Ghazali reminds us that it would be impossible for us to really understand the deeper reasoning and true meaning of these orderings of ritual actions. But if we go back to the way the Prophet ﷺ did things, it becomes easy for us. We copy his way. How could the actions of the Prophet ﷺ, in all his movements, be different or apart from a special standard, code or order? Because the Prophet ﷺ learned these ablutions from the angel Gabriel, when we do them, we are near to God ﷻ. There are *two* different ways that we can all do things. Can you guess what they are?"

Bilal ventured, "We can do things in order or haphazardly – out of control – in any which way! That happens to me a lot. It feels chaotic and sloppy."

"Exactly, Bilal," praised Father Hamza. "Think of all the peaceful, humble, pious people you see and how they do things. Calmly and with presence, no?"

Abdullah imagined his parents, grandparents, teachers at school and Haj Abdullah, moving rhythmically and beautifully through these orderly forms of worship. He tried to picture each one of them doing everything in different ways! It was not a peaceful image.

"My dear children, as you know the Blessed Prophet ﷺ is the

perfect example of how to do everything. Following the ways *he* ﷺ did things is called the '*sunna*'. The nearer our actions and inner thoughts are to this blessed norm and order, the further away they are from being haphazard and neglectful. By following in this way, we are being closer to the saints and the prophets. Isn't that clear and wonderful?"

Abdullah added, "And in that way we are closer to God because the Prophet ﷺ himself is very close to God. And this is what we want in the deepest part of our hearts."

Bilal continued, "That's why we are learning to polish our hearts. We think that because we are children, we have many, many years ahead of us – all the time in the world. But we are also learning that our lives in this world are shorter than we think. We are so blessed, Father, to have your guidance and the help of so many dear elders and Imam al-Ghazali, in getting us on our way. Habits are easy to make, so we may as well take on good habits rather than bad ones. We are learning about inner and outer purity and this gives us a solid foundation for having beautiful characters and leading wonderful lives. *Al-HamduLiLah.*"

The Book on the Mysteries of Purity For Children

The Book on the Mysteries of Purification and Its Importance – being the third book of the quarter concerning worship from the *Revival of the Religious Sciences* – is here completed with praise to God and His Help. May blessings and salutations be upon our beloved Master and God's Prophet Muhammad and upon his family.

This book will be followed by the *Book on the Mysteries of Prayer and Its Importance*. All praise be to God Alone, and may He send blessings and salutations upon our beloved Master, Muhammad.

Imam al-Ghazali

AL-GHAZĀLĪ

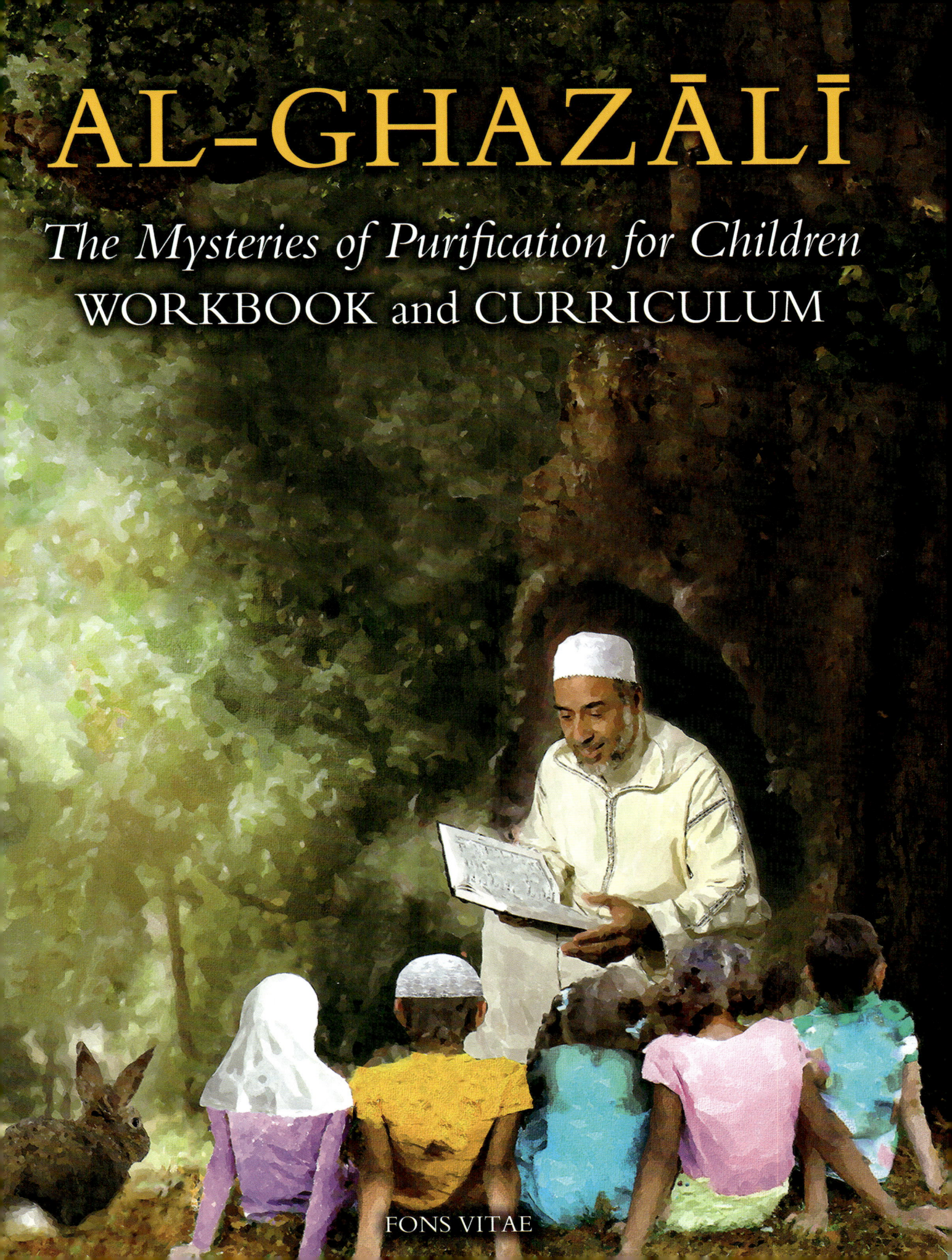

The Mysteries of Purification for Children
WORKBOOK and CURRICULUM

FONS VITAE

Workbook
for
Imam al-Ghazali
The Book of the Mysteries of Purification
and Curriculum for Children

بِسْمِ اللَّهِ الرَّحْمَٰنِ الرَّحِيمِ

ﷻ-subhanahu wa ta ala: Glory be to He

ﷺ-salla-llahu alayhi wa sallam: Peace and blessings be upon him

ؑ-alayhi-s-salam: Be upon him peace

؏-alayha-s-salam: Peace be upon her.

ؓ-radia-llahu anhu: May God be pleased with him

Dear Children, Families, and Teachers,

There is something for each age group in the pages to follow. Parents can simplify the questions and activities for the very small; some of you might like to color; others can do the questions and activities on their very own. Ideas for further activities and a school curriculum conclude this volume.

The curriculum activities and crafts are listed chapter by chapter. Parents will want to do these at home with the children as they are lots of fun and will ensure the children have begun practicing the virtues in an unforgettable way. The core teachings of each chapter are also presented here along with relative Quranic passages and hadith as well.

Everyone is invited to the website: ghazalichildren.org to meet with your global brothers and sisters, to participate in contests, to submit your own ideas for activities, for curriculum, updates, and anything else. Simply enjoy the many resources provided for both children's entertainment and for parents and teachers as well. Many of the activities, core teachings, and films will be helpful in the classroom. Join in on a regular basis.

The Publisher

Workbook
for
Imam al-Ghazali
The Book of the Mysteries of Purification
and Curriculum for Children

FONS VITAE

The Book of the Mysteries of Purification For Children Workbook

First published in 2017 by
Fons Vitae
49 Mockingbird Valley Drive
Louisville, KY 40207
http://www.fonsvitae.com
Email: fonsvitaeky@aol.com

© 2017 Fons Vitae
No part of this book may be reproduced
in any form without prior permission of
the publisher. All rights reserved.

Printed in Canada

Illustrations and cover by Ithar Abusheikha
Line drawings by Farida Khalil
Curriculum team led by Rebekah Seda
including Farah Abid, Jannah and Sarah Ahmed,
Siraj Mowjood, and the Peace Terrace School

Please frequent www.ghazalichildren.org for updates,
competitions, meeting one another and much more.

Table of Contents

Prologue: Gathering in the Special Garden	7
Chapter 1: *Wudu*	11
Chapter 2: The Four Levels of Purification	17
Chapter 3: The Magical Tree House and the Stations of Faith	21
Chapter 4: Back in the Special Meeting Place	27
Chapter 5: Things That Are Clean and Some That Are *NOT*	31
Chapter 6: Washing with Water	35
Chapter 7: The Toothbrush	37
Chapter 8: Beginning *Wudu*: The Mouth	41
Chapter 9: The Nose	45
Chapter 10: The Brightened Face	47
Chapter 11: Shining Hands and Forearms	51
Chapter 12: Top of Your Head, Ears and the Neck	55
Chapter 13: Finally Your Feet	59
Chapter 14: More Helpful Tips to Know	63
Chapter 15: Breakfast at Grandmother's	67
Chapter 16: In What Way Should We Try To Look Beautiful?	71
Chapter 17: The Order In Which We Do Things	75
A Parent-Teacher's Manual: My Shining Heart Curriculum and Activities for the Book of Purity	81

The Book of the Mysteries of Purification For Children Workbook

What wonderful things could Haj Abdullah be explaining to the children?

Prologue
Gathering in the Special Garden

1. What are some useful things you learned in Books 1 and 2?

Name three:

a. _____
b. _____
c. _____

2. What wondrous ideas did the children wish to share with Haj Abdullah?

3. When something difficult or upsetting happens in your life, how can you use it to polish your own heart? Give an example.

4. What kind of plan or map does Imam al-Ghazali give you to help polish your heart?

The Book of the Mysteries of Purification For Children Workbook

5. When do the fish in the sea and even the ants ask God ﷻ to bless you? Is it when you are teaching by being a good example?

6. How are you doing with arguing? Bragging?

7. When the Imam wrote in his life story "Up, up and away! If not NOW, When?!", what was he trying to say to himself?

8. How many animals can you find in the drawing? Please add your own ideas and color.

Imam al-Ghazali

The Book of the Mysteries of Purification For Children Workbook

What is the scholar saying to the mysterious, elderly visitor?

Chapter 1
Wudu

1. Tell what happened in the story about the scholar and the old man who asked, "What is *wudu*?" What happened when the scholar discovered who this elder *really* was? What did the scholar learn?

2. What did *you* learn from this story? What can you do while you wash in *wudu*?

3. Draw the scholar sitting at the feet of the town's holy man.

The Book of the Mysteries of Purification For Children Workbook

4. What might happen if you were playing or chatting with a friend and then you simply went directly to pray without having been given *wudu* to do in between playing and praying? What would that feel like?

5. Draw someone clean on the outside, but with a dirty heart on the inside. How would that feel?

6. If purification or being clean on the outside of your body is half of faith, what is the other half?

Imam al-Ghazali

7. There are two ways of doing things, outer and inner. Give an example of each in your daily life activities.

One example might be:

A child in your class has been left out by others. You might choose to become a friend, and be kind. You can do this nice thing for different reasons:

a. to make people like you better; or
b. to please God ﷻ by doing what is Right.
Below write or tell about an example of each of these in your daily life activities.

8. Are you excited about learning the inner, secret meanings of *wudu*? Why?

The Book of the Mysteries of Purification For Children Workbook

Write under the drawings of the scholar the words that best describe him:

patient	kind	sharing
friendly	bragging	gossiping
angry	humble	impatient
proud	helpful	mean

Imam al-Ghazali

When the scholar went to visit the village elder, what did he learn? Circle the correct words.

anger	silence	greed
humility	peace	spying and prying
pride	bragging	to pray while doing *wudu*

Color in the drawings above and add your own details.

The Book of the Mysteries of Purification For Children Workbook

As the boy washes his face, what might he be asking God ﷻ ?

Chapter 2
The Four Levels of Purification

1. To review, the four levels of Purification are:

   a. Cleaning any dirt off the body – whatever breaks *wudu*.
   b. Purifying the different parts of the body from doing wrong things so they can instead be filled with worship – (like the mouth and what it says)
   c. Purify the Heart from low character so it can shine perfectly.
   d. Purify one's innermost being from *anything* concerned with the lower self. Those able to reach this level are the prophets and saints.

   Give an example of something you can do for levels a – c.

   a. _____
   b. _____
   c. _____

2. What happens when you remove some faults? What takes their place when they are gone? Give an example.

3. Get a glass of water and put dirt in it. Then empty it and refill it with clean, pure water. Which one can be used to wash with? If a person is dirty inside, do you like to be with them?

The Book of the Mysteries of Purification For Children Workbook

4. You have learned many things that you should not do. How do you change your habits? What does following the *sunnah* mean in your life?

5. What is possible to do after *wudu* is made?

6. Draw a house. Make the door shining and clean. Draw trash inside the house. What happens if you only clean the outside of your body?

Imam al-Ghazali

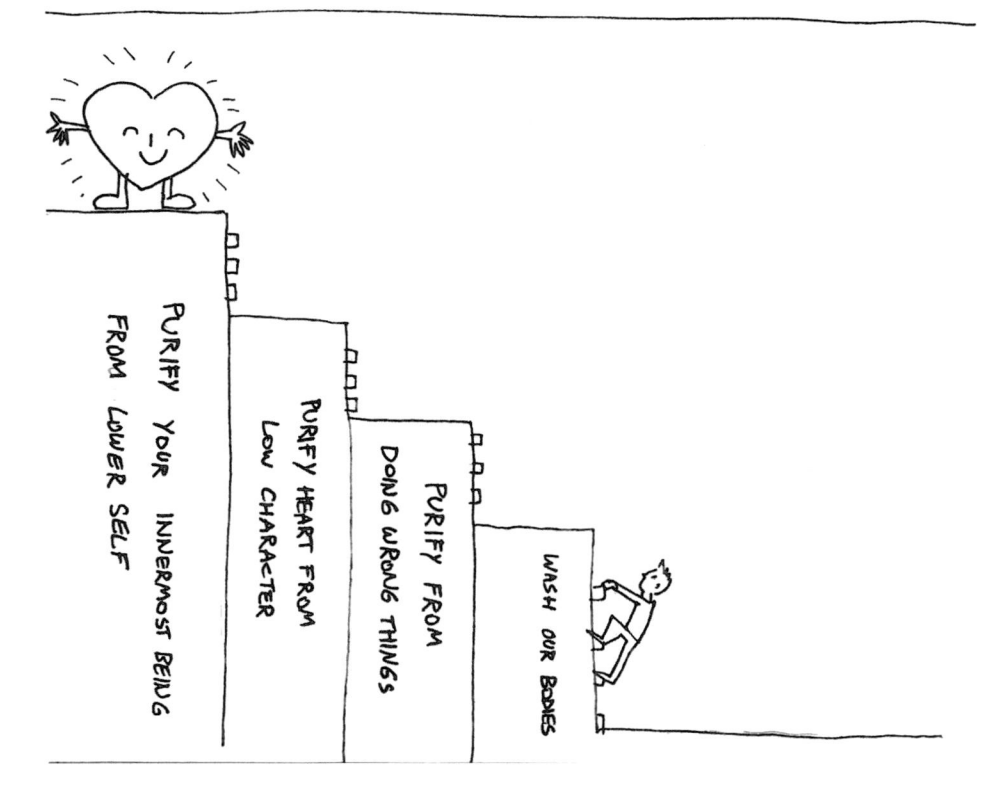

*it's so far...
how do I...?*

The Four Levels of Purification

Describe climbing up levels 1, 2, and 3.

The Book of the Mysteries of Purification For Children Workbook

What is magical and special about this tree?

Chapter 3
The Magical Tree House and the Stations of Faith

1. Draw the Magical Tree in the center of the garden. Add four platforms, but make the top one very, very hard to see.

2. Pretend that the steps from the ground to the first platform are like the steps you learn ABOUT HOW to make *wudu*. Next, add wooden boards to be used as steps nailed on to the bottom of your tree trunk and continuing up to the second platform.

The Book of the Mysteries of Purification For Children Workbook

3. Draw a small figure on top of the first platform. This person, who has been taught how to make *wudu*, has (choose one):

   a. Learned a new game to play
   b. Cleaned the dirt off his body – whatever has broken *wudu*
   c. Learned how to count

4. Draw Platform 2. What are you doing now that you have reached the second station?

Which are true?

   a. Practicing climbing on a ladder
   b. Doing the inward parts of *wudu* as you wash each bodily part.
   c. Asking God ﷻ to forgive you for naughty things you have done and help you do better.

Imam al-Ghazali

Color and add steps going from station to station. What are you learning on the steps from the ground up until Platform 1? Choose two.

   a. How to climb trees
   b. How to polish your heart
   c. Lessons ABOUT HOW to do *wudu*

The Book of the Mysteries of Purification For Children Workbook

5. While rinsing your mouth, what could you be asking God ﷻ?

6. If Platform 3 stands for Polishing your Heart so it shines brightly, what are some things you are doing already to reach that special place inside you of good character?

7. What are some kinds of things you have learned about the Prophet ﷺ, or very saintly people that could be found on Platform 4, at the highest level of faith?

8. Grandfather mentioned something that the Prophet ﷺ said: "God looks not at your bodies or your wealth but rather at your hearts and your works" (Muslim, *Sahih* (4650, 4651); Ibn Maja, *sunnan* (4233))

What do you suppose is meant by this hadith?

9. In the time of the Prophet ﷺ, people dressed humbly and focused on making their heart shine. Many people today focus more on making their outward bodies look good. Draw a picture of each type of person and draw their two types of hearts, too.

The Book of the Mysteries of Purification For Children Workbook

What kind of little girl is this?

Chapter 4
Back in the Special Meeting Place

Haj Abdullah told the children that Polishing the Heart is like climbing up a high mountain, which is not easy. Pretend you are a hero or heroine going on an important journey, but difficulties await you. If you are polishing your heart, what are some of the problems you meet?

1. Draw some pretend dragons and trolls, and write on each one some bad thing about your lower false self that your True, Real Self wishes to slay.

2. In the story, little Abdullah said, "What fun it is having something REAL to do as we go about our daily lives." What *real* thing is he speaking about? Can you give an example? Can you draw an example?

3. What are some reasons we should remove our shoes before prayer? Draw what might happen if we wore our shoes inside a mosque or place of prayer.

Imam al-Ghazali

4. Circle the words below that are most like the dragons and trolls you wish to remove from yourself. Color this picture.

backbiting	being angry	not helping	being mean
bragging	arguing	not sharing	being greedy
hypocrisy	spying and prying	being selfish	

The Book of the Mysteries of Purification For Children Workbook

What might Omar be asking Haj Abdullah?

30

Chapter 5
Things That Are Clean and Some That Are *NOT*

1. All the many things that are not alive, like rocks and tables, are all pure and clean but there is one thing that is NOT alive but is impure. What is it? Why do you think it could be considered not pure?

2. What two animals are not considered clean? One of them is a great protector and friend of human beings and has many excellent qualities.

3. Usually things that are dead are thought to be not clean, except for five. Find and circle these five pure things in the list.

a dead bug	a dead fish	a dead worm	a dead locust
a dead cat	a dead person	a dead bird	a dead mouse

4. When we perform the *rite* of prayer, we need to have a special kind of purity in order to be *ritually* clean. When we play sports or with our toys, do we need to be *ritually* pure? Why or why not?

The Book of the Mysteries of Purification For Children Workbook

5. If you cut your finger and blood gets on your clothes, just when you are about to pray, what should you do?

6. There are some wet substances that come out from the human body. Circle the ones that are considered pure:

tears
  when we cry

perspiration
  when we are hot

saliva that keeps our
  mouths wet

blood
  when we are cut

what comes out
  when we use the toilet

mucous
  in our noses

7. Draw the five pure ones – like two eyes crying.

Imam al-Ghazali

If this little girl has a bit of dirt on her dress, does she need to wash it off before she prays? She loves to play outside and she loves to pray out under the sky as well. What about you? Color this picture. Will you make the sky at the time of dawn, noon, afternoon, sunset, or night?

The Book of the Mysteries of Purification For Children Workbook

By adding a cup of juice to this spring, has the little girl made the water too impure to use for wudu?

Chapter 6
Washing with Water

1. It is all right to play in muddy water. But in order for water to be used for making *wudu,* it needs to be *ritually* pure, so that it may be used for worshipping God ﷻ. Water cannot be used to make *wudu* if something has touched it that changed any of three things about it. Name these.

   a. _____
   b. _____
   c. _____

2. What would happen if you threw a small teacup of chicken soup into a large pool of clean water?

Underline what is true: The water from the large pool of water...

   a. The water would still be pure and could be used for *wudu.*

   b. The water is no longer clean and pure.

   c. The water absorbed the small cup of soup which then vanished.

3. Draw a cat sipping out of a pot of water. Is that water still clean enough for making *wudu*?

The Book of the Mysteries of Purification For Children Workbook

What is Haj Abdullah holding?

Chapter 7
The Toothbrush

1. What did people use to brush their teeth before modern toothbrushes? Draw one.

2. What is one important reason the Prophet ﷺ gave for using the toothstick?

3. One prayer said after you brushed your teeth is better than _____ prayers without brushing.

4. Imam al-Ghazali mentions that the Prophet ﷺ didn't want to make things difficult for his followers. For that reason, he didn't ask that everyone do what before each prayer?

The Book of the Mysteries of Purification For Children Workbook

What would be a good reason to brush your teeth before every prayer and *wudu*? Have you ever tried to use a *siwak* stick? Color and put in many extra details.

5. Draw yourself brushing your teeth. Indicate the two directions best used in brushing.

The Book of the Mysteries of Purification For Children Workbook

When you rinse your mouth three times, what does Imam al-Ghazali suggest that you ask God ﷻ ?

40

Chapter 8
Beginning *Wudu*: The Mouth

1. Ablution, or *wudu*, is not complete if you forget to say what phrase?

2. Also, for your *wudu* to be acceptable, you must try to keep your intention in your mind and not let your mind daydream. What two things can you say that you are intending?

    a. _____
    b. _____

3. How many times do you rinse out your mouth? _____

    Do you use your right or left hand? _____

    Draw your hand lifting water to your mouth.

3. While rinsing out your mouth, Imam al-Ghazali suggests that you say, "O God, help me in the recitation of your Book and to remember You abundantly." What are three other things you could ask God ﷻ about what you have said in the past?

41

The Book of the Mysteries of Purification For Children Workbook

4. When you are speaking to your friends or your siblings, what are five things you can say that would please God ﷻ?

a. _____

b. _____

c. _____

d. _____

e. _____

5. List five things you are sorry you said.

a. _____

b. _____

c. _____

d. _____

e. _____

6. Draw some good things you can put into your mouth.

The Book of the Mysteries of Purification For Children Workbook

What could the SMELL of these flowers in this garden remind the children of?

Chapter 9
The Nose

1. What did Imam al-Ghazali suggest you ask for while you sniff in refreshing water?

2. How many times do you rinse your nose? _____

3. Draw a boy blowing the water out of his nose. What can he ask God ﷻ to protect him from when he does this?

4. Draw one or all of the four rivers that flow in Paradise. Add flowers as well! And what about drawing the fountain in the center?! When we see rivers and fountains and flowers, they are *ayat,* or signs. What do they remind us of?

The Book of the Mysteries of Purification For Children Workbook

What prayer might Khadija have SAID as she rinsed her face?

46

Chapter 10
The Brightened Face

1. Draw on outline of a face showing all the places the water must reach. How many times is the face rinsed?

Now draw rays of light around the face to remind you of the excellent prayer to say as you wash, "O God, brighten my face with Your Light when the face of Your Friends are brightened…"

The Book of the Mysteries of Purification For Children Workbook

2. Draw a pair of eyes and show with arrows how your index finger should clean around them.

3. Draw something beautiful that you love to look at. Allah ﷻ is The Beautiful and He ﷻ loves Beauty.

Imam al-Ghazali

4. List five regretful things you pray that your eyes do not do or look at.

   a. _____

   b. _____

   c. _____

   d. _____

   e. _____

5. Name five beautiful things you can see or look for with your eyes.

   a. _____

   b. _____

   c. _____

   d. _____

   e. _____

The Book of the Mysteries of Purification For Children Workbook

What is Khalid asking God ﷻ as he washes his hands three times?

Chapter 11
Shining Hands and Forearms

1. What special thing, when you reach the Next World, will you notice has happened to all the parts of the body that you carefully washed when you made *wudu*? Draw an outline of a person's body and draw what will happen.

2. What can you do during *wudu* to *increase* the shining light that will shine from all the parts you wash?

The Book of the Mysteries of Purification For Children Workbook

3. Is it better even to wash above your elbows? Why?

4. What can you ask God ﷻ as you wash your right and then left hands three times?

  - You ask God ﷻ to present the book listing all the good things you did before you died in your _____ hand.
  - You ask God ﷻ to protect you from receiving this book in your _____ hand or behind your back.

5. What are some good things you *do* in your daily life?

6. What are three things you are sorry you have done in your past and want to avoid from now on?

  - _____
  - _____
  - _____

Imam al-Ghazali

Color this little boy doing his *wudu* and add some lovely details. Write something he could be asking God ﷻ as he rinses his hands and forearms up past the elbows.

The Book of the Mysteries of Purification For Children Workbook

What could HEARING the beautiful sounds of the ocean and the birds remind the children of?

Chapter 12
Top of Your Head, Ears and the Neck

1. After wetting your hands, put the tips of your fingers touching each other and then wipe over your head from where your forehead hair begins all the way down the neck. Do this three times. Now, draw your hands with the fingertips touching, and then show what you do.

2. In the prayer you say while you are wiping the top of your head, you ask Allah ﷻ to cover you with His blessings and Mercy while forgiving all your wrongdoing. You also ask Him, as you wipe your head, to give you shade beneath His Throne in the Next World. Draw a throne giving shade.

The Book of the Mysteries of Purification For Children Workbook

3. There are three things to do when you purify your ears. What do you do?

- Place each index finger in _____
- Use your thumbs to _____
- Use the palms of your hands to _____

How many times do you do this? _____

4. While washing you ears, what might you ask God ﷻ to help you with?

- _____
- _____
- _____

What things are not good to hear?

- _____
- _____
- _____

What are some wonderful ways you can use your ears?

- _____
- _____
- _____

5. I like to listen to:

- _____
- _____
- _____

6. Draw an ear and draw some things it loves to hear.

7. After wiping the crown of your head, hair and ears, each three times, there is something left to do but only ONCE. Show how this is done. Make a big drawing.

8. What can you ask God ﷻ as you wipe your ears?

- _____
- _____
- _____
- _____

The Book of the Mysteries of Purification For Children Workbook

Hasan's feet have taken him to help his Mother, who is very pleased.

Chapter 13
Finally Your Feet

Draw an outline of your two bare feet with spaces between the toes.

Number the toes in the order they are washed. See number 3 below for help.

The Book of the Mysteries of Purification For Children Workbook

1. Starting with your right foot, pretend to wash over it three times using your left hand.

2. Now, using your left index finger, pretend to wash between each of the toes on the drawing of your right foot, starting with the little toe on the far right.

3. Before wiping over the left foot, look at the numbers on the toes 1-10 you wrote on your drawing, starting with the little toe of the right foot first. The big toe of the left foot will be #6 and the left little toe will be #10. In what order will you clean your ten toes? It is like going up and down a tiny hill.

4. Prayer while purifying you feet could be:

Dear Allah ﷻ, Please keep my feet from taking me to places that would not please You, like:

- _____
- _____
- _____

Thank You, God ﷻ, for directing my feet to:

- _____
- _____
- _____

5. How can these inner prayers said while you are doing *wudu* help to polish your Shining Heart? Give two ways:

- When you wash your mouth_____
  _____
- When you wash your ears_____
  _____
- When you wash your hands _____
  _____

6. There is a prayer you can do, looking up towards the heavens, after you finish *wudu*. Imam al-Ghazali tells us that this prayer will rise up from you to just beneath God's Throne and will go on and on praising Him, and will be there for you in the Next World. It has four parts:

    a. Shahada
    b. Ask forgiveness
    c. And ask for guidance
    d. Praise God when you first awake and just before you go to sleep.

It's a lot to remember, but which one of these four can you say easily? a., b., c., or d.?

7. You can make a poster for your bathroom that reminds you of the order and prayers of *wudu*…until you learn it by Heart! Make an outline here and then prepare a big one that you can hang up.

The Book of the Mysteries of Purification For Children Workbook

If a king were coming to visit, would you only polish the door and leave the inside a total mess? What about your own insides? Shiny or messy?

Chapter 14
More Helpful Tips to Know

1. Would it be a good idea to do more than three washings during *wudu*?

Is doing more washings better?

2. What is a reason NOT to talk or have a conversation with someone while you are doing *wudu*?

3. What is the difference between inner and outer *wudu*?

4. What matters to Allah ﷻ the most?

The Book of the Mysteries of Purification For Children Workbook

5. Draw both a house and an outline of a person. Make the outsides of each shine and the inside full of rubbish.

| Person | House |

Imam al-Ghazali

6. How do you feel when the outside or inside of you seems dirty?

If you invited a king to visit your home, would you only polish the door and leave ugly rubbish inside? How is this like doing *wudu* only with outward movements and leaving your mind and heart thinking about something else? What does Allah ﷻ care about most? Your Heart?

The Book of the Mysteries of Purification For Children Workbook

Did Bilal do his wudu just before going to bed? How can you tell?

Chapter 15
Breakfast at Grandmother's

1. Draw the children having breakfast at Grandmother's. Or draw what she cooked, something you like for breakfast?

2. There is a hadith that says that if you offered two bowings, or *rakahs* of prayer after making a good *wudu* and your mind was not wandering, you will finish that prayer as pure as the day when _____, and also, God ﷻ will forgive you for _____ _____!

3. What are some situations where doing your *wudu* could be very, very difficult? Like when water is hard to find or you are in a very cold place.

What can happen if you do *wudu* anyway?

4. Imam al-Ghazali mentions that if you repeat your *wudu*, even a few times, Allah ﷻ will add _____ good deeds to your list.

5. Draw a person, who has finished his *wudu*, with bad doings and sins leaving, streaming out from his or her eyes, nose, mouth, face, hands, and feet. Even from under the eyelids and toenails!

6. How many gates or ways of entering Heaven are there? _____

If you say the *shahada* after you do your *wudu*, which gates can you go through to enter the Heavenly Garden? Draw these gates and garden.

7. Draw yourself lying in bed at night with your shining, golden heart. Why *might* it be a good idea to go to sleep just *after* being purified by *wudu*?

The Book of the Mysteries of Purification For Children Workbook

What beautiful things are the children SEEING that remind them of Paradise?

Chapter 16
In What Way Should We Try To Look Beautiful?

1. Since we are all teachers, what is the best way we can teach?

What are three things you could teach that are good and beautiful? Tell how you would do that.

- _____
- _____
- _____

2. One of Allah's ﷻ holy names is *The Beautiful*. Name three beautiful things you can see that remind you of Him and Paradise.

- _____
- _____
- _____

3. If you see something bad or ugly, it can remind or even warn you NOT to do the same thing. Name two bad or ugly things you would not want to do.

- _____
- _____

4. Everything we see can be a sign or reminder, and a lot of special reminders come up each day. If you notice a dead bird or bug, what can that remind you about?

5. If you see a person being kind and generous, what does that remind you to do?

71

The Book of the Mysteries of Purification For Children Workbook

6. What does the low, false, *not* true self want you to do?

7. Tell about something that your Real, High, Luminous Self wants you to do?

8. What will you do *today* to polish your Shining Heart? Tell a story about this or do a drawing.

Imam al-Ghazali

His room always smells of incense

His clothes and hands always so neat

His gaze so sincere

افضل محبوب الحر
ما يدخله في قبره
و يوانسه فيه
فما وجدت خير
الاعمال الصالحة
فأخذتها محبوبا
لي لتكون سراجا
لي في قبري...

His words full of Light

Sitting with him always reminds me of Heaven.

If you were sitting in silence with Imam al-Ghazali, what might he be teaching you just by the way he was? What would you like to copy? "His clothes and hands always so neat. His gaze so sincere. His words full of Light."

The Book of the Mysteries of Purification For Children Workbook

"A beautiful Light will reach the places the ablutions reached."
Muslim 250

Chapter 17
The Order In Which We Do Things

1. Draw whichever is considered more noble – the hand or the foot. Why do you think that might be?

2. Draw or trace around your right hand. Which of the fingers is considered to be most noble and why? What special thing does *this* finger get to do during prayer?

The Book of the Mysteries of Purification For Children Workbook

3. Now draw both hands and put R on the right hand and L on the left. First, put your fingertips together, thumbs on thumbs and little finger on little finger. Look at the index finger on the right hand. Moving in the right direction, you will reach the right little finger. If you are moving in a circle, which finger is next?

4. The toenails have a different order because no toe has the special use the way the index finger does during prayer. Draw your 2 sets of toes and number the nails in the order they will be trimmed. Write R on the right foot and L on the left foot. The order is quite different from the fingers.

5. Which is easier: cleaning your hands and feet or cleaning and polishing your heart? Why?

6. How did we find out about how many times we should do something and in what order?

7. What would it be like if everyone did whatever number of washings they felt like and in any order? Which do you prefer, and why?

8. How does the habit of doing things in a certain order bring you nearer to Allah ﷻ and His Prophet ﷺ?

9. How can doing *wudu* in all the ways you have been learning help to polish your heart?

10. Make a new checklist/*wudu* chart of all the things you will try to say or do each time you make your *wudu*. You can hang it on the wall of the bathroom. You can add your drawings to help.

Imam al-Ghazali

Color the room and rug where Abid often prays and LISTENS to recordings of the Qur'an.

The Book of the Mysteries of Purification For Children Workbook

Of key importance to the success of these teachings:

Imam al-Ghazali concluded his *Book of Knowledge* by explaining that we are all teachers and that people copy one another. The Prophet ﷺ said that the whales and the ants ask God to bless good teachers and the angels stroke them with their wings. It is of utmost importance that both parents and teachers not only read the books but also model the virtues which have been presented in an easy and useful form as these accessible texts based on the Imam's profound teachings. If you read a story to a child about the ugliness of anger or gossip, and then you are angry or gossip yourself, which example is stronger and easier for the child to imitate? On the other hand, if you catch yourself and say out loud, "Oh dear! I acted wrongly!" the children will have a valuable and concrete lesson in self-observation and self-correction. Whatever we say or do we must ask ourselves, "Would I like someone to copy this?"

My Shining Heart Curriculum and Activities
A Parent-Teacher's Manual for The Book of the Mysteries of Purification
Table of Contents

Teaching Methods for Parents and Teachers	83
Goals	84
General Teacher Supply List	84
General Student Supply List	85
Teacher Etiquette	85
Rules of Written Work	85

My Shining Heart Program

Curriculum Overview	86
Classroom Tools	87
Comprehension Tools	92
Prologue: Curriculum Guidance	92
Chapter One: Curriculum Guidance	92
Chapter Two: Curriculum Guidance	93
Chapter Three: Curriculum Guidance	93
Chapter Four: Curriculum Guidance	94
Chapter Five: Curriculum Guidance	95
Chapter Six: Curriculum Guidance	96
Chapter Seven: Curriculum Guidance	98
Chapter Eight: Curriculum Guidance	99
Chapter Nine: Curriculum Guidance	100
Chapter Ten: Curriculum Guidance	102
Chapter Eleven: Curriculum Guidance	103
Chapter Twelve: Curriculum Guidance	105
Chapter Thirteen: Curriculum Guidance	105
Chapter Fourteen: Curriculum Guidance	107
Chapter Fifteen: Curriculum Guidance	108
Chapter Sixteen: Curriculum Guidance	109
Chapter Seventeen: Curriculum Guidance	110

Fons Vitae invites parents and teachers to send us their own creative ideas for curricula and activities which will help children practice what they are learning in their daily lives. Your comments and suggestions will help Fons Vitae design future curricula and make any needed adjustments to future editions of this volume (www.ghazalichildren.org).

You will notice that several of the activities are repeated in every chapter. If a child practices or, for example, draws on his or her heart-drawing once, it will not become a conscious part of his or her life. By repeating these activities over and over again, it is hoped that the child will feel so familiar and at home with these ideas that they will become permanent habits.

A Parent-Teacher's Manual of Activities and Curriculum
To be adjusted creatively according to age groups

Teaching Methods for Parents and Teachers

Children will easily recognize and understand the truths of each teaching from Imam al-Ghazali. What is of utmost importance is that these lessons are reinforced by actually being practiced on a regular basis. In life, what we do over and over again quickly becomes a habit and the way we naturally do something. In this curriculum, we present traditional teaching methods such as review questions, crafts, and songs, but we also introduce a new method of play-learning in the spirit of prophetic instructions to let children play. Playing games and play-acting virtuous qualities is a fun and effective way for children to change their reflex reactions through repetition and allow those virtuous qualities to become second nature. For example, they need to first play "*not* sharing" to experience how awful it feels. If we simply counsel children, "Don't brag!" "Don't gossip!" "Don't be greedy!" and so on, it is too abstract. They need to play-act these vices to truly understand their wrongness from within. And then they must practice sharing in play-acting, over and over again, until it becomes easy for them and an experienced pleasure – even fun! The success of the Ghazali Children's Series will depend upon the children being encouraged by parents and teachers in creative and enjoyable ways to practice all their learning on a regular basis, and begin to see life through this perspective.

Fons Vitae would be more than grateful if any of the play-acted skits performed at home by children were to be captured on video. We are finding that children who visit our website (ghazalichildren.org) are particularly drawn to these skits, as they can see other children practicing the same virtues and reading the same stories that they are. This shows them that they too can write and perform their own skits to practice what Ghazali teaches them.

We ask teachers and parents to use the ghazalichildren.org site as a useful classroom tool and as home entertainment – the core teaching videos help make deep ideas clear.

Also on this site will be found pictures which clarify the making of such craft supports as the *Wudu Spin the Wheel Game*.

Curriculum Delivery

- The Ghazali Children's curriculum is intended to be a habit-forming program that builds upon itself. It includes daily practice, weekly class meetings, and monthly community service activities that are repeated in order to form and reinforce good habits. Class time consists of short and light-hearted readings, reflection time, arts/crafts, and games.

- This curriculum is intended for children ages 7 to 13 years old. The Lexile level of the *Book of Purity* is appropriate to be read aloud by an adult to any age group. Children who are reading on grade level could read the *Book of Purity* to themselves if they are mid-year 3rd grade or higher. The reading materials and curriculum could potentially be simplified for younger children and adjusted for older adolescents at your own discretion.

- Supplemental activities are presented for each chapter but the heart of this program is achieved by following the "My Shining Heart Program" found below.

- The timing and amount of material to be delivered at once is up to the teacher, although you will notice that this curriculum is presented as if the students were meeting at least weekly. Meeting at least once weekly is recommended for the sake of habit building.

The Book of the Mysteries of Purification For Children Workbook

- Try to deliver the curriculum in the sequence presented in the *Book of Purity* (unless otherwise noted) because the curriculum builds upon itself. Some activities correlate to more than one chapter, and some chapters are very short so you may choose to combine chapters.
- Encourage reverence for the Earth by using natural and biodegradable materials when possible. Order recycled paper and card stock in bulk to reduce price. Other materials to consider include beeswax crayons, wool felt, wood, quality paper, and cotton fabric.
- Teachers should engage the students with real life experiences and examples, give instructions, supervise discussions, and help the student when needed.
- Please create your own activities too and post them on www.ghazalichildren.org for the whole community. We simply request that you keep the activities habit-forming and fun!
- Be creative in your teaching approach. Reach out to Fons Vitae if you need help, and please encourage your students to frequently visit http://www.ghazalichildren.org/ for illustrated guides to the activities.

Goals

Teachers and students will:
- Read the text.
- Use comprehension tools presented in this curriculum.
- Answer and discuss questions in the Workbook and the related Qur'an passage and hadith.
- Follow the in-class schedule of activities.
- Participate in daily-life activities.
- Participate in community service activities.
- Be role models of good character to others around them.
- Learn the basics of the rituals of *wudu*.
- Appreciate the ritual of *wudu* in relation to being more cognizant of their thoughts, actions, and words and how they relate to their spiritual hearts.

General Teacher Supply List

- *Book of Purity* (for Adults), *Book of Purity for Children*, *Workbook for Book of Purity for Children*, large item to write on such as a dry erase board, large flipping paper pad on an easel, or chalkboard with corresponding writing materials, and definition board, which should exhibit new words found in the most recent and present chapters (can be a separate chalkboard or paper pad).
- Materials for *Wudu* Spin the Wheel Do-It-Yourself (DIY) craft
- Materials for *Wudu* Charades and Pictionary DIY craft

A Parent-Teacher's Manual of Activities and Curriculum

General Student Supply List

- *Book of Purity for Children*, *Workbook*, composition journal(s), pencils, colored pencils.

Teacher Etiquette

- We must demonstrate to our children that we are applying the Ghazali Children's Series to ourselves and that we are willing to participate in the learning activities. For every learning activity, we strongly recommend doing exactly what the children are expected to do, yourself.

- Make the lessons in this Series a regular conversation in your family/class, and/or share the lesson plans with the families of the children in your class clearly requesting that they incorporate the Series into their family life. (Parents will be included among those referred to as "teachers" in this manual.)

- You are key to nourishing the children's motivation as you gather them to learn in a *supportive* and *non-judgmental* environment, providing positive reinforcement for their efforts.

- Have realistic expectations based on each child's developmental level in helping the students perform virtuous habits and putting into practice what they have been taught. Young children vary considerably in their understanding of questions and taking part in discussions.

- Be patient and encourage your student to reach his/her maximum potential and praise them often in their efforts to develop good character. Remember, you may not see all of the positive results of this Series until the children have grown into adults, but God-willing ﷻ it is making a positive impact!

Rules of Written Work

- Children may write in their *Workbook* or answer *Workbook* questions in their own journal.

- You may photocopy pictures in the *Workbook* for coloring or allow children to color in their own *Workbook*.

- Encourage students to keep their written work orderly and neat. Writing with a pencil instead of a pen may be neater.

- If using reflection journals, encourage timely updates each time a discussion takes place.

- Students should write in paragraph form and stress the importance of keeping all work free from blemishes.

The Book of the Mysteries of Purification For Children Workbook

My Shining Heart Program
Curriculum Overview

Class Schedule

1. Before class, write the essential question from the chapter under study on the board for children to ponder during class. Also, use the definition board for key words. Use the core lesson as a guide for yourself and for checking understanding at end of class. Analyze the children's discussion, writing, artwork, etc. in relation to the core lesson. The core lesson, essential question, and definition board words are found under the curriculum sections and activities for each chapter ahead. Their purpose is described under the section "Comprehension Tools" below.

2. Initiate class with *dua'a*.

3. Begin each class with "Guided *Wudu* Contemplation Time," in which the children are asked to silently reflect upon their behavior over the past week while making the movements of *wudu*. Silence is essential during this time except for your voice. For the order of making *wudu*, ask the children to visualize cleansing their body of bad deeds, and being filled with light and good deeds. Detailed instructions and a sample script of Guided *Wudu* Contemplation Time is below under "Classroom Tools."

4. Read and discuss a chapter from the *Book of Purity for Children*, examine and work together to answer workbook questions. Read and discuss the related Qur'an/Hadith provided under each chapter's curriculum section. Read the Qur'an/Hadith as part of the workbook time, allowing children to copy the passage into their journals.

5. At every meeting, take time to play a game that emphasizes the connection between the ritual of *wudu* and the Spiritual Heart. Playing these games is essential for the children's learning. Instructions for *Wudu* Charades, *Wudu* Pictionary, and *Wudu* Interactive Skits are found below.

6. Complete other supplemental activities mentioned under each Chapter Curriculum Guidance or of your own creation.

7. Play the "*Wudu* Spin the Wheel Game" in which the children will spin a game wheel to select which body part to observe for the upcoming week. Ask the children to perform at least seven good deeds in relation to the selected body part. Ensure that each child knows the basics of how to wash the selected body part. Create *Wudu* guidance/reminder cards (ideally laminated) with basic instructions for how to wash the specific body part including the associated prophetic *dua'a* or a simple *dua'a* in the child's own language. Give the card to the child to post on the wall next to their sink at home, and ask them to refer to this card when practicing *wudu*. Once the *dua'a*s are learned and the cards become numerous, hole punch them and keep them on a ring.

8. End each class with *dua'a*. Let the children take turns speaking from their hearts.

Daily Home Practice

1. Instruct children to post their *Wudu* guidance/reminder cards next to the sink where *wudu* will be practiced, or attach them to the body part of focus on the Life Size Body Drawing (see ahead).

2. Ask the children to look for seven opportunities to either correct a bad deed and/or practice good deeds with the selected body part over the week to come. At the following session, the children should be given a chance to report on their experience, not necessarily just sharing what good deeds they did, but truly reflecting on the experience including struggles.

A Parent-Teacher's Manual of Activities and Curriculum

Monthly Practice

1. Initiate minimum monthly community service projects. Examples include working in teams to donate toys and clothing, cooking food for those in need, and/or visiting the sick/elderly. The teacher is essential in assisting the children in planning and arranging these repeated activities, and making sure the children keep them up. This helps instill generosity, mercy, and patience in daily life.

2. It is important that teachers read ahead in the materials so that they can adequately plan for these activities.

Classroom Tools

Guided *Wudu* Contemplation Time

Objectives:

- Repeat the order and proper movements of *wudu* with the children in an unimposing and spiritually-oriented manner.
- Emphasize the importance of quiet time for self-reflection.
- As you will repeat this activity at every meeting time, you can begin simply and then make it more advanced with time.

You can lead this contemplation time without water, but it would be beneficial to give the children their own personal water bowls/basins at least once. Sit outside on the grass or somewhere the children will not be reprimanded for splashing a bit. Here is a suggested script that you can say all at once or break up into smaller segments. Vary as you see fit. You, the teacher, will demonstrate the proper movements to perform for each body part:

1. Sit with the children in a circle. Say, "Now that we have made *dua'a*, let's practice our *wudu* and take some time to reflect on ourselves over the past week. This is a silent activity so you will think about your answers to yourself."

2. "Say "Bismillah" to yourself and begin to wash your hands, interlacing your fingers and washing tops and bottoms. Think about washing away any action you have done with your hands that you are not proud of. Once clean, your hands are filled with light; what good can you do with your hands now? Answer silently to yourself." Let the children pretend that they are washing their hands as if they are making *wudu* as you are saying this.

3. "Wash your mouths like this, pretend to rinse and release the water. What is one thing you wish to say better in the future? Wash away what you said in the past, and now your mouth is filled with light. What do you wish to say now?"

4. "Rinse your nose and release the water quietly. Think about the sweet smell of *jannah*, infinitely more beautiful than even the best smell you have ever experienced on earth."

5. "Wash all parts of your face and eyes. Imagine washing away any mean or sour facial expression you have had, and replacing it with a smiling face filled with light."

6. "Wash your hands and arms like this, making sure to reach behind your elbows and washing down to your hands, interlacing your fingers. Think of something you might have done with your arms and hands that you are not proud of; what can you replace it with?"

7. "Wipe your heads like this. What are some bad thoughts you want to wash away? Now they are replaced with light so that you can think good thoughts."

8. "Wash your ears like this. What are things you have listened to that you are not proud of? What can you replace it with?"

9. "Now wash your right and then left foot like this. Wash in between your toes and back to your heels. Have your feet taken you into any situation that you're not proud of? What kinds of activities would you prefer for your feet to take you toward? Imagine all the dirt being replaced with light."

Variations:

Eventually add in the prophetic *dua'a*s that should be said during each part of the *wudu*. You can spend as much time as needed on each *dua'a* before going to the next one. If the children do not know Arabic, make sure they learn the meaning of each *dua'a* in their native tongue. Use the printable found on the Ghazali Children's website for an easy reference to these *dua'a*s.

Life Size Body Drawing

The Life Size Body Drawing is a craft that will help you achieve three teaching objectives:

Objective 1: Review the order of each body part washed in *wudu* and the number of times it is washed.

Objective 2: Help visual and tactile learners brainstorm good and/or bad deeds that can be committed with the body parts washed in *wudu*. After brainstorming, write the children's ideas on post-it notes to place on the life size body drawing and keep your own list as well. Use this list to make game cards for *Wudu* Charades, *Wudu* Pictionary, and *Wudu* Interactive Skits.

Objective 3: Teach the sunnah *dua'a*s or simple prayers in the children's own language related to each stage of *wudu*. Post-it notes or other paper materials can be attached without damaging the drawing.

Instructions for creating Life Size Body Drawing:

Materials you will need:

- Large paper
- Washable markers, crayons, or colored pencils

1. Ask children to pair up and trace each other's bodies onto the paper; tape them all togeher into one large body.
2. Paint the tracings with water color or decorate as desired, although not necessary.
3. Prepare to use the drawings in a way that will allow you to make changes. For example, cover it with contact paper and plan to use pencils/erasers, post-it notes, tape etc.
4. Hang the drawings on the wall as space allows.
5. Use the tracings in conjunction with the *Wudu* Spin the Wheel Game to meet the three learning objectives above.

***Wudu* Charades / *Wudu* Pictionary / *Wudu* Interactive Skit Games**

Learning about the deeper meaning of *wudu* through games allows children to experiment with self-observation and self-correction in a fun way. Repeat one of the following three games as part of your class schedule every time you meet so that the children have sufficient time to explore all the concepts and make long-lasting mental and spiritual connections. Do not rush the games, and allow the children to make mistakes and figure out solutions for themselves.

First step: Brainstorm Heart and Body Connections

Using the list of good and bad deeds (associated with each body part) created by the children above, discuss how the good or bad deeds may be associated with a character trait in the spiritual heart. One example might be: the eye can envy, or the mouth might brag. Use the vices/virtues of the Caution List that the children learned about in the *Book of Knowledge* (see below). For example, jealousy in the spiritual heart may encourage someone to misuse their hands to hit, steal, or type a mean message. Write down the children's ideas. This set of ideas will be referred to if/when children need help coming up with ideas while playing the suggested games.

Caution List:

1. Envy is opposite to Wanting Good for Other People
2. Lying is opposite to Honesty
3. Being a Know-It-All is opposite to Humility and Letting Other People Be Right
4. Arguing is opposite to Agreeing with Others and Being Peaceful
5. Anger is opposite to Peacefulness and Patience
6. Hate is opposite to Love
7. Bullying is opposite to Being Friends with and including Everyone
8. Gossip/Backbiting is opposite to Respecting Everyone (even when they are not around)
9. Greed is opposite to Generosity
10. Pride is opposite Humility
11. Making Excuses is opposite to Being Responsible
12. Prying and spying is opposite to Minding Your Own Business
13. Bragging/Showing Off is opposite to Modesty and Humility
14. Being Two-Faced/Hypocrisy is opposite to Integrity/Truthfulness
15. Doing Too Many Things is opposite to Concentrating on What You are Doing
16. Wasting Your Time is opposite to Making Good Use of Your Time
17. Ignorance is opposite to Seeking Knowledge
18. Ingratitude is opposite to Gratitude
19. Meanness is opposite to Kindness

Second step: Create Game Cards

Make two piles of note cards, ideally of different colors. On one set, write out the vices/virtues from the Caution List. On the second set, list each body part washed in *wudu*.

Instructions for Playing *Wudu* Charades:

This version of charades is modified to allow the players to speak, but they should not make specific verbal reference to their selected vice/virtue and body part. Divide the children into two teams or play as one group. If breaking the group into teams, one player from the first team will choose a card from each pile (body part washed in *wudu* and virtues/vices) and show it to the other team and one other acting partner. The players from the first team will quickly brainstorm a skit that demonstrates how the vice or virtue could be done with the body part. Their own team will try to guess both the vice or virtue and body part the skit represents. If the actors have trouble developing an example for their selected vice/virtue and body part, then you can refer them to the Heart and Body Connection list you created above, provide your own ideas and assistance, or allow them to choose different game cards.

The Book of the Mysteries of Purification For Children Workbook

Two minutes are usually sufficient for guessing, but you may alter the time limit. Allowing the use of props will make it easier to guess. You should let the guessers know when they have guessed correctly. If any of the guessers makes the correct association within the time limit, then their team wins a point. Alternate until each team member has had an opportunity to be an actor. You will eventually cover all of the virtues/vices and body parts as you repeat one the three games (Charades, Pictionary, Interactive Skits) each class period.

Instructions for Playing *Wudu* Pictionary:

Drawing and interpreting drawings allows children to learn through symbolism. Divide the children into two teams or play as one team. The first players draws a card from each stack (body parts washed in *wudu* and virtues/vices) and then thinks of a way to demonstrate this through a drawing. The first player shows the cards to the other team and/or you before beginning to draw. The drawing should be of a simple story that demonstrates "Heart and Body Connections" as above. The drawing should not be just of the body part, but of course, it may become easily obvious in the drawing. Each player and his or her team have five minutes for the player to make his/her drawing and for the team to guess. Any drawing materials are suitable including colored pencils/paper, markers/dry erase board, chalk/chalk board, etc.

Instructions for *Wudu* Interactive Skits:

Pair the children up into groups of two or three. Each group will draw one card from each pile (body parts washed in *wudu* and virtues/vices). Instruct the children to develop a three to five minute skit which demonstrates a "Heart and Body Connection" of their selected game cards. The skit should demonstrate a vice, and once the children have acted out this vice, they will pause. (If a group has trouble developing an idea, refer to the list the children brainstormed, provide an idea for them, or allow them to draw cards again.) Once the actors have paused, they should then ask the other children to reflect on the problem presented in the skit, and explain how to fix the situation. Encourage the children to first ask the actors questions about how they are feeling and what they want out of the situation. Then, the children can give advice on how to fix the situation. The actors should go with the other children's ideas, and everyone will assess as a team if it helped the problem to be solved. Your job is to help guide the observing children to correct the dilemma presented in the skit.

***Wudu* Spin the Wheel Game**

The spin wheel game is a DIY craft that will point to pictures of different parts of the body washed during *wudu*. It will be used for each chapter of the *Book of Purity for Children* to add playfulness to learning the movements and *dua'a*s for *wudu*. Only one game wheel is needed for the whole class to share. Each child spins the game wheel and the arrow will land on one body part that they can focus on using during the next week. For example, if the student lands on the ear, he/she pays special attention to *listening* to good things and turning his/her listening away from bad things. (Good and bad deeds should be reviewed with parents and teachers). During this week, the student also utilizes the *Wudu* guidance/reminder cards to practice the specific movements of ear washing in *wudu*, and the related *dua'a*.

Instructions for DIY *Wudu* Spin the Wheel Game with foam board:

For a visual example, see ghazalichildren.org and http://apples4bookworms.blogspot.com/2013/01/wheel-of-wonder-diy-spin-wheel-game.html

Materials you will need:
- Sticky velcro circles (or squares)
  - If you don't have velcro, use a sticky material like putty or tape

- Construction paper/felt/fabric, various colors, cut into eight "pizza slice" sections for hands, mouth, nose, face, arms, head, ears and neck, and feet
- Glue sticks or rubber cement
- Paperclip
- Piece of packing tape
- Razor blade or cutting tool
- Images for each body part washed in *wudu* as noted above (drawings or printed)
- Two foam boards/laminated card stock paper/real wood, one will be cut into a circle and the other will remain a square/rectangle

1. Trace out a circle on one foam board. Use a razor blade to cut out the circle.
2. Cut out 9 different colors of construction paper (one for each body part), and then arrange and glue to the foam board.
3. Before poking holes through the foam board and threading the paperclip through, place the little square of packing tape on the spot you will poke. This will keep the paperclip from tearing up the construction paper while it spins.
4. Place the circle foam board on top of the square/rectangle foam board. (Center the circle foam board.) Unbend the paperclip and poke a hole through both foam boards exactly where the packing tape is placed. Thread the paperclip through both boards and then bend back the paperclip on each end.
5. Attach pictures of body parts towards the top of each "pizza slice." If using velcro, place a velcro circle towards the top of each color. The velcro on the board should all be on the same side, such as the fuzzy side. On the back of your body part pictures, place the scratchy side of the velcro circles.
6. Draw an arrow on the back foam board so that, when the game wheel is spun, the arrow will indicate which section of the spin wheel has been selected.

Instructions for DIY *Wudu* Spin the Wheel Game with vinyl music record or disc:

Materials you will need:
- Sticky velcro or other sticky craft material that can be stuck and unstuck
- Construction paper, various colors, cut into 8 "pizza slice" sections for hands, mouth, nose, face, arms, head, ears and neck, and feet
- Rubber cement or other strong glue
- Thumbtack
- Images for each body part washed in *wudu* as noted above
- Vinyl music record (craft vinyl records can be purchased in craft stores – they are intended for children's art, and are not real music records) or any heavy disk – like a large tin can lid.

1. Attach construction paper to vinyl record with rubber cement or a strong glue.
2. Place a velcro circle towards the top of each "pizza slice." The velcro on the board should all be of the same side, such as the fuzzy side. On the back of your body part pictures, place the scratchy side of the velcro circles. Attach pictures to record by means of velcro or a different adhesive material.

The Book of the Mysteries of Purification For Children Workbook

> 3. Attach a vinyl record to the wall by placing a thumb tack through the center hole. Indicate on the wall a point to select the body part of focus. Spin the wheel and see which body part is closest to wall point.
>
> *See the ghazalichildren.org for visuals please.
>
> ## Comprehension Tools
>
> - The Core Lessons serve as checkpoints for verifying that children understand the basic message of the chapters, but are not meant to be easy summaries so as to diminish the process of learning through stories and playing. Before moving on to a new chapter, the teacher should review the Core Lesson(s) in the previous chapter with the students.
> - The Essential Questions are meant to be open-ended, and can be used in class discussion and/or for personal journals in class or at home.
> - The Definition Board is essential for helping children understand the language found in the *Book of Purity*. Use it every session to assist the children in developing their vocabulary and understanding of the material.

Prologue: Curriculum Guidance

Activity: Ghazali Children Series Check-In

Ask the children to reflect on any changes in their lives based on the *Book of Knowledge* and the *Book of Belief*. Some sample questions may include:

1. How am I am different after reading the first two books of the Ghazali Children's Series?
2. What is one example of a change I see in myself now versus the beginning of the program?

Now ask the children to draw a picture or write a short poem or paragraph to express their answers. Share these with the class in Circle Time.

Discuss the good True Self and the "lower false self," and about being the kind of "teacher" you would like to be for others by example.

Chapter One: Curriculum Guidance
Refer to class schedule in Curriculum Overview box

Core Lesson: Purification is both outward and inward.

Essential Question: Why should I try to understand the meaning behind Islamic rituals, such as *wudu*? How does my attitude about worship change when I learn about the deeper meaning of rituals?

Definition Board: ritual, purification, meaning, inward, outward, ablutions, revered, humility

Qur'an Passage related to Chapter Story: Ask a child to read aloud part of Surah 5 Verse 6 during workbook time: "O ye who believe! When ye prepare for prayer, wash your faces, and your hands (and arms) to the elbows; rub your heads (with water); and (wash) your feet to the ankles."

Activity 1: Create *Wudu* Spin the Wheel Game

Create this craft in class with students or beforehand. See preceding Curriculum Overview for instructions.

Activity 2: Old Man and the Scholar Mini-Play

Determine roles and provide props for children to re-enact the short story of the old man meeting the scholar. Paper bag puppets could also be made and used. Provide basic *dua'a* examples for the child play-

A Parent-Teacher's Manual of Activities and Curriculum

ing the old wise man when he explains the real meaning of *wudu* to the scholar. In that way, s/he can be introduced to the way of using the *dua'a*s. However, the *dua'a*s will be learned gradually over the following classes. See printable on Ghazali Children's website for an easy reference.

Chapter Two: Curriculum Guidance
Refer to class schedule in Curriculum Overview box

Core Lesson: Purification has four levels: purifying one's body from impurities, purifying one's body from sinful actions, purifying one's heart from low character, and purifying one's soul, which is the level of the Prophets, peace be upon them all, and saints. *Wudu* helps us to remove what is bad and replace it with what is good on each of the levels.

Essential Question: Why is making *wudu* beneficial for me? Encourage critical thinking to give more meaningful answers than just, "So that I can pray."

Definition Board: level, impurity, character, soul, presence, sacred, character

Qur'an Passage related to Chapter Story: Ask a child to read aloud part of Surah 33 Verse 4 during workbook time: "And God has not placed two hearts in any person's breast."

This is not referring to the physical heart that pumps blood, but to the spiritual heart that seeks to be polished and empty of everything but God's Presence ﷻ. There is only one of these Hearts, not another seeking lower things.

See instructions above in Curriculum Overview for the following activities.

Activity 1: Create Life Size Body Drawing

Activity 2: Create Games (Charades, Pictionary, Interactive Skits)

    First step: Brainstorm Heart and Body Connections

    Second step: Create Game Cards

Chapter Three: Curriculum Guidance
Refer to class schedule in Curriculum Overview box

Core Lesson: Muslims must remind themselves that the ritual of *wudu* is one level that must lead to the greater spiritual levels. We should learn to do it properly, but be careful not to be distracted/overwhelmed by the details so that we forget out about cleaning our Hearts.

Essential Question: What harm could come to us if we just focus on the ritual of *wudu* and forget about its deeper meaning and use?

Definition Board: station, platform, shimmering

Qur'an Passage related to Chapter Story: Ask a child to read aloud part of Surah 24 Verse 24 during workbook time: "On the Day when their tongues, their hands, and their feet will bear witness against them as to their actions."

Discuss what this could mean in daily life.

Activity 1: Climbing the Steps of the Treehouse

    Rather than build a treehouse, make four stations along the floor (maybe large cardboard boxes). Let the children act out the story in which one can play the part of the grandfather. The others will ask questions about the four levels of faith and everyone will try to answer these. After they answer, they can move from one station to another and explain what they learned on a previous platform in order to

The Book of the Mysteries of Purification For Children Workbook

go up – or move – to the next station.

Activity 2: The Four Levels of Purification Box

This activity provides a tangible demonstration of the four levels of purification - how moving through each level brings you closer and closer to having a glittering, shining heart. For this activity, you will need a cardboard gift box (or a box of similar size), glitter, glue, a brush, and pretty paper to wrap around the outside of the box. Use crinkle paper for the inside of the box, paper flags, and sand or spices to look like dirt.

Step 1: With a little craft glue, coat the inside of both the top and bottom of your box. Generously sprinkle the coated areas with glitter and set aside to dry. You may also add a heart inside the box to emphasize that the True Heart is shining and pure.

Step 2: Crumple the craft paper in your hands until it appears slightly weathered. Set it aside.

Step 3: Fill your box with the paper crinkles, then place the lid on top. On the paper flags, write vices you wish to polish away from your heart, like "being lazy," or "complaining," or "not helping my mom." Stick the paper flags on the lid using a little tape if necessary.

Step 4: Now wrap the entire box in the crumpled craft paper. Sprinkle this wrapped box with sand, or another dirt-like substance (you can just use dirt, but spices and sand may be cleaner).

How to play: The first level of purification is to clean your physical body from anything that prevents you from making prayer. Brush off the sand or spice "dirt" from the wrapped box. You have completed the first step of purification.

The second level of purification is to cleanse your body parts from committing any sinful acts. Remove the crumpled craft paper. You have completed the second level of purification.

The third level of purification is to remove the blemishes that blotch your shining heart. Remove the paper flags. You have completed the third step of purification.

The fourth level of purification, the level of the prophets and saints, is to cleanse your heart of every trace of your lower self. Remove the crinkle paper from the box and marvel at the beautiful, shining heart. Explain this perfect Shining Heart is inside EVERY person but just gets dirt on it. Explain that this is the ultimate goal of life – completing the fourth step of purification – which has been reached by saintly people and prophets. Even if we are unable to reach this level, this is the aim.

Chapter Four: Curriculum Guidance
Refer to recommended class schedule above in Curriculum Overview

Core Lesson: We must understand the special obstacles or difficulties in our lives, and that they are sent to polish our hearts. We must be careful not to criticize and judge others and not to pay so much attention to outer details that we forget the inner Heart.

Essential Question: What are some of your own dragons or trolls you wish to get rid of?

Definition Board: noble, obstacles, hero/heroine

Qur'an Passage related to Chapter Story: Assign a child to read aloud part of Surah 25 Verse 32 during workbook time: "Those who reject Faith say: "Why was not the Qur'an revealed to him all at once? Thus (is it revealed), that We may strengthen thy heart thereby, and We have rehearsed it to thee in slow, well-arranged stages, gradually."

(This verse can be used to illustrate the point that our journey to Allah ﷻ and polishing our Hearts occurs in stages, one step at a time.)

A Parent-Teacher's Manual of Activities and Curriculum

Activity 1: Fairy Tale Variation to *Wudu* Charades

Following the instructions for playing *Wudu* Charades or *Wudu* Interactive Skits in the Curriculum Overview above, explain to the children that today's class will have a fairy tale theme. When developing their game skits, the children should think in terms of fairy tale stories and characters. For example, at first one of the actors pretends to be a dragon/troll/ogre that represents a fault. The observing children should guess what vice the fairy tale villain represents such as anger/bragging/greed, etc. The actors could then demonstrate how they can overcome the villain by doing the opposite, and thereby pretend to turn into a magic prince/princess/hero/heroine.

Activity 2: Interpretive Fairy Tale Art and Storytelling

Use the children's fairy tale stories to develop art and/or written short stories/comic strips. For example, if a story involved a dragon and sword then provide art materials by which to create a dragon mask and paper sword. After playing Charades, they can write on the mask "selfish," and on the sword "generous." Display the children's artwork in your classroom and share it with parents encouraging them to support and continue the theme at home.

As an alternative, provide large sheets of paper and art utensils for children to develop a comic strip of their fairy tale story. Divide the sheet of paper into equal-sized squares and ask the children to draw each scene of their story.

Chapter Five: Curriculum Guidance
Refer to recommended class schedule above in Curriculum Overview

Core Lesson: Our Revealed Law excuses certain kinds of impurity or dirtiness. Ritual purity is based on ease and not hardship.

Muslims should have a basic knowledge of things and substances that are ritually clean and those that are not:

- All non-living things are pure and clean except for alcohol or substances that alter the mind.
- Unclean living creatures include dogs, pigs, and dead creatures. Five exceptions to unclean dead creatures include human beings, fish, locusts, apple worms, and insects.
- Unclean substances that come from our bodies include digestive waste and blood (except for small amounts of blood).
- Clean substances that come from our bodies include tears, breast milk, sweat, saliva, and mucus.
- Soil on clothing or on shoes (after washing off what one can) is not ritually impure.

Essential Questions: When do I need to be ritually clean? How do I feel when I know that Allah ﷻ has made His Revealed Law easy for me to follow?

Definition Board: Revealed Law, impurity, ritually clean, rite

Qur'an Passage related to Chapter Story: Ask a child to read aloud part of Surah 5 Verse 6 during workbook time: "God does not want to burden you; He wants to make you pure, and to complete His favor to you, that you may be grateful." Discuss and copy into workbooks or journals.

Activity 1: Variation for *Wudu* Interactive Skit: Hassan and Hussein's Winning Method

Share with the children the story of Hassan and Hussein (may Allah ﷻ eternally bless them), in which the two boys saw an older man making ablutions incorrectly. Instead of scolding him, they asked him to watch each of them make *wudu* and be a judge as to who made *wudu* the best. In this way, the man realized his own mistakes without being humiliated. Ask the children to act out this scenario.

The Book of the Mysteries of Purification For Children Workbook

Next, brainstorm with the children scenarios in which a fellow Muslim is performing *wudu* and does not know about which things are ritually clean and unclean. Acting out the scenarios as part of *Wudu* Interactive Skit time, instruct the children to first demonstrate correcting the other Muslim in an impolite manner. How did this feel? How might "pride" and "resentment" be related to this scenario? (The harsh teacher may feed his/her own pride by behaving this way, and cause his/her fellow Muslim to resent him/her.)

Now, ask the children to think of a gentle way to help correct the situation. How does this feel to the one teaching and the one being corrected? Ask what they have learned from this and to act out the same inspiring idea in other situations they can make up.

Activity 2: Mini-Treasure Hunt for Clean Objects

Ask the class to go outside and collect objects which are not alive, but clean, and put them on a table for everyone to see. Which non-living substance is not on this table and why? (Answer: Alcohol.)

Activity 3: Puppet Theater Play "The Man and His Arrow"

Share the following story with the children to illustrate how focusing only on the details of the *wudu* can make one miss the whole intended purpose of the ritual:

"A man was wounded in battle, but he didn't let his friends draw the arrow out of him. First he wanted to know who the archer was, what he looked like, and where he was standing when he shot the arrow. He wanted to know the type of bow and the length of the arrow. As he discussed all these things, he died," (*When You Hear Hoofbeats Think of a Zebra*, p. 3).

Ask the children to make up stories like that from their own daily lives. "What would happen to me if I only focused on asking questions about the details when:

- "I fell off my bike and cut my chin badly?"
- "I heard someone calling for help who couldn't swim and I only…"

Chapter Six: Curriculum Guidance
Refer to recommended class schedule above in Curriculum Overview

Core Lesson: Be sure that the water we use for *wudu* doesn't have a changed color, smell, or taste.

Essential Question: What kind of water is needed for *wudu*?

Definition Board: liquid, overwhelm

Qur'an Passage related to Chapter Story: Ask a child to read aloud Surah 15 Verse 22 during workbook time: "And We send the winds fertilizing, and cause water to descend from the sky, and give it you to drink. It is not ye who are the holders of the store thereof."

Activity 1: Water as a Mercy Class Mural

Materials you will need:
- Large item to draw on such as paper, blackboard, dry erase board
- Art utensils such as paint/paint brushes, colored pencils, crayons, chalk, etc.

Brainstorm various sources of water with the children, and discuss their flow cycles. Divide the children into small groups to create an art mural which demonstrates the flow cycle of water with its many sources. At the top of the mural(s), write "Water is a Mercy" or another special message concerning water.

Activity 2: Properties of Water Demonstration

Fill a large bowl with water. Add a small amount of colored water in order to demonstrate water's

A Parent-Teacher's Manual of Activities and Curriculum

ability to absorb smaller impure amounts.

Activity 3: "Can we make wudu with *any* water?" Demonstration

Materials you will need:
- 6-8 small to medium sized bowls, each filled with water and numbered
  - 2-3 of your bowls should have only food coloring and another 2-3 should have only essential oils or white vinegar.
  - 1-2 bowls should have some sprinklings of spices, apple cider vinegar, loose tea, or glitter.
  - 1-2 bowls should have only clean water.
- Sticky notes
- Water
- Food coloring
- Essential oils/white vinegar/clear-colored liquid perfume
- Spices/apple cider vinegar/glitter/loose tea/pieces of leaves

Place the bowls on a large table. Have the children inspect and smell the water in the bowls. Then ask them which bowls contain water that can be used for *wudu* and which bowls contain water that *cannot* be used for *wudu*. The "contaminants" should be obvious to make the purpose of this activity clear from the purpose of Activity 2 above, which demonstrates that a small amount of "contaminant" added to a large amount of water will not disrupt the water's purity for making *wudu*.

Activity 4: Sing "Mercy Like the Rain"

Sing together as a class, and consider a final performance to share with family and/or create a video for the Ghazali Children website where these songs may also be found under Book 3

https://m.youtube.com/watch?v=sEsEHthTqlI

Here is version performed by children:

Kids performing Mercy like the Rain

https://m.youtube.com/watch?v=dd_b3v9huVA

Lyrics to "Mercy Like the Rain"

Mercy like the rain is falling down
Mercy like the rain is falling down
Can you feel the rain is falling down, falling down?
Mercy like the angels in the rain
Mercy like the sun, the moon, the stars
Blossoming flowers, bearing fruits
Showing us the greatness of Allah
Mercy like the faith that shines within us
Mercy like the prayers that Allah answers
How it gives purpose to our lives
Helping us strive for paradise
Mercy like the smile for one another
Mercy like the kindness for each other
O how it takes sadness from our hearts

The Book of the Mysteries of Purification For Children Workbook

> Spreading God's love throughout the world
> Mercy like the Messenger of Allah
> Mercy like the Qur'an from Allah
> Truthful, generous, wise and kind
> Bringing Allah's words to mankind

Chapter Seven: Curriculum Guidance
Refer to recommended class schedule above in Curriculum Overview

Core Lesson: The main goal of following a sunnah of our Messenger Muhammad ﷺ is to grow in love for him ﷺ. Using a siwak before each prayer is a special sunnah of our Beloved Messenger ﷺ with great reward. We try to follow our Messenger Muhammad ﷺ not just in our outward behavior but also in our inward behavior. The shortcut to a pure Spiritual Heart is having great love for the Messenger ﷺ because when you connect your Heart to his ﷺ, you are connecting your Heart to the most, sound pure heart of all.

Essential Question: What kind of relationship do I want with God's ﷻ Messenger ﷺ?

Definition Board: messenger, sunnah, isnad, pathway, preferred, community

Hadith related to Chapter Story: Ask a child to read aloud the following hadith during workbook time: "Verily your mouths are pathways of the Qur'an, so sweeten them with the toothstick." Ask the children to copy this hadith into their workbooks or journals.

Activity 1: Your Friend, the Siwak:

Bring in good quality *siwaks* for the children to see and try out. Let the children keep them for use at home. Does it feel different compared to using a regular toothbrush and toothpaste? Caution: some vendors sell poor quality *siwaks* that will give the children a negative first experience. Try to avoid this. If no *siwak* sticks can be found, toothbrushes can be used instead.

Activity 2: Video: A Gift that Keeps on Giving from the Prophet Muhammad ﷺ

As an engaging story, share with the children that the Prophet Muhammad ﷺ received knowledge of how to perform the *Wudu* from the Archangel Jibril who brought it as a message from Allah ﷻ. We try to follow the way the Prophet ﷺ did *wudu* in the same order, copying his example.

However, some very learned scholars of a high spiritual status have been tested for accuracy in performing *wudu*. Share this video with the children about a scholar who has *ijaza* in *wudu*. Explain that his example goes back to the Prophet Muhammad ﷺ, and has been verified. Thus, when we watch him, we are watching a very close example to the way the Prophet Muhammad ﷺ actually performed *wudu*:

https://www.youtube.com/watch?v=kR6sUbfaev4

Activity 3: Allah ﷻ Speaks to Me through His Beloved Messenger Muhammad ﷺ

Create a visual for the children to see the chain of transmission from Allah ﷻ to Archangel Jibril to the Prophet Muhammad ﷺ to the child. It can be a wall hanging, a page in their journals, the cover of a folder they will be using in this Series, a bookmark, etc. The point is that they will see this representation of the chain of transmission and remember this special connection to God ﷻ through receiving His knowledge. At www.freeislamiccalligraphy.com you can download free printouts of beautiful Islamic calligraphy with Allah's ﷻ name or the name of His Beloved ﷺ. Or you can make calligraphy yourself or use decorative English words. You may print out pictures of the children ahead of time to represent the child's position at the bottom of the chain of transmission or simply write out his/her name.

A Parent-Teacher's Manual of Activities and Curriculum

Activity 4: Sing *Tala 'al Badru Alayna*

Encourage love for the Messenger ﷺ through singing. There are many versions of this traditional song, but Yusuf Islam presents a high-quality version that includes the English translation and thus may be more meaningful to the children. Discuss the lyrics and learn the song with the children. Bring in drums to encourage a special music time in the classroom.

Link to song: https://www.youtube.com/watch?v=BM0ZQy0TPm0

Lyrics for *"Tala al Badru 'Alayna"* by Yusuf Islam

Tala al Badru 'Alayna
Min Thaniyati-al Wada'
Wajaba Shukru 'Alayna
Ma da'a lillahi da'

O the white moon rose over us
From the valley of Wada'
And we owe it to show gratefulness
Where the call is to Allah

Ayyuha-al Mab'uthu feena
Ji'ta bi-al amru muta'
Ji'ta sharafta-al Madeenah
Marhaban ya khayra da'

Oh you, who were raised among us
Coming with a word to be obeyed
You have brought to this city nobleness,
Welcome best caller to God's way

Tala al Badru 'Alayna
Min Thaniyati-al Wada'
Wajaba Shukru 'Alayna
Ma da'a lillahi da'

Activity 5: The Islamic *Isnad* Tradition

Inviting a guest speaker to a classroom or home school environment can be very refreshing. In this case, look for an individual in your community who has been granted permission through an *isnad* chain to teach an Islamic topic. Ask the speaker to tell his/her story to the children and demonstrate how an *isnad* chain works, recite some beautiful Qur'an, and hold a Q&A session. While the goal is to emphasize to the children that they are each recipients of religious knowledge, it will hopefully be inspiring to the children to know that they could become fine people or even scholars of special status who teach others.

Chapter Eight: Curriculum Guidance
Refer to recommended class schedule above in Curriculum Overview

Core Lesson: *Wudu* begins with the *basmallah* and intention and the rinsing of the mouth three times. It has two levels of meaning.

The Book of the Mysteries of Purification For Children Workbook

Essential Question: What can you do while rinsing your mouth that will help polish your Heart?

Definition Board: suggestion, intention, abundant, decision, access, moist

Hadith related to Chapter Story:

Discuss with your children the following hadith during workbook time:

> "A man came to the Prophet, may Allah bless him and grant him peace, and said, 'Messenger of Allah, the laws of Islam have become too many for us, so [give us] a means of access to which we can cling which is comprehensive.' He said, 'Let not your tongue cease to be moist with the remembrance of Allah, mighty is He and majestic.'"

Then remind the children to think about this when they wash their mouths during *wudu*.

Activity 1: *Wudu* Charades / Interactive Skits / Pictionary with Focus on Speech

Following the class schedule, use the *Wudu* games to focus on correcting negative speech with virtuous speech. For example, the children act out skits where they pretend to speak badly, but then catch themselves, and correct what was said. Ask the children to use ideas from the workbook list for this chapter. After playing the games, the children should choose one statement from the list to practice saying that week.

Activity 2: Gossip! Telephone Game

Ask the children to stand in a line. Whisper into the first child's ear a long, detailed story. The first child then whispers his/her version of the story into the second child's ear and so on. The more times the story is passed, the more it may become distorted. The last person shares what s/he heard out loud for the group to assess. Discuss how this game relates to gossip.

Activity 3: Break Before You Backbite

As a part of the *Wudu* interactive skits or separately, teach the children to ask themselves four questions before they say anything about anyone. If the answer to any of these is "no" then it is likely backbiting or idle talk:

1. Will I be able to say this in front of the person I am talking about?
2. Am I absolutely sure that it is true?
3. Is what I am about to say kind?
4. Is what I am about to say necessary?

Activity 4: "The Power of Words" Demonstration

Inform the children that you will teach them about the "power of words" through a symbolic lesson. Carry a small bag of sand or another fine substance like salt outside. Tell the children, "These grains of sand or salt are our words. We can use words to help people or to hurt people. They are very powerful." Sprinkle the sand/salt on the ground around you and look at these grains carefully. Now ask the children, "Can you pick up the sand/salt and put it back in the bag? Even if you are able to clean some of it, are you able to clean all of it? Why not?" "How does this relate to the words we speak? Is it easy to take words back?" A child once compared trying to take back words – which we regret having said – to trying to get toothpaste back into the tube!

Chapter Nine: Curriculum Guidance
Refer to recommended class schedule above in Curriculum Overview

Core Lesson: Rinsing out the nose is a sunnah of our Beloved Messenger Muhammad ﷺ that can remind us of Paradise.

A Parent-Teacher's Manual of Activities and Curriculum

Essential Question: When you rinse your nose with water, what should this remind you of?

Definition Board: relatives, scented, refreshing, musk, fragrance, spoil

Hadith related to Chapter Story: Ask a child to read aloud the following hadith to be copied into workbooks or journals during workbook time:

> Narrated by Abu Huraira: Allah's Messenger ﷺ related, "Allah ﷻ said, 'I have prepared for My pious worshipers such things as no eye has ever seen, no ear has ever heard of, and nobody has ever thought of.'" (Bukhari)

Remind the children that the scent of Paradise is infinitely sweeter than anything they have experienced in this life.

Variation for *Wudu* Contemplation Time: At the time for rinsing the nose, ask the children to imagine Paradise and hear the bubbling of the Fountain of Life. Ask what they see, smell, hear, feel, and taste. Tell the children that as wonderful of a place they can imagine that heaven will be, Allah ﷻ says it will be even better than we could have ever dreamed of!

Activity 1: Dreaming about Heaven – It's better than you can imagine!

The purpose of this activity is to create internal motivation for purifying one's heart, and to help make rewards in the afterlife more meaningful. Depending on the age of the children, and their ability to write, lead an activity asking the children to imagine heaven and think about all the things they would want. Suggested activities include writing a page in their journal, making artwork by drawing, painting, or cutting out beautiful photos for a collage, or simply sitting with another classmate and sharing their dreams of heaven.

Activity 2: Sensory Demonstration to Understand Hadith

Ask a child to read aloud the following hadith:

> "The example of a good companion and a bad one is like the bearer of musk and the worker with fires. A bearer of musk would give you some, you might buy some from him, or you might enjoy the fragrance of his musk. The worker on the fires, on the other hand, might spoil your clothes with sparks from his bellows, or you get a bad smell from his activity." (Bukhari)

Bring in good quality essential oils (*itr/attar*) to class and let the children take turns smelling them (without rubbing it on their skin). Ask for one volunteer to try on his/her favorite scent on his/her forearm using a generous amount. Now the first volunteer will rub his/her forearm against the forearm of a second volunteer. As the children share this experiment, ask them to take note of how easily the scent transfers to others and to objects you might touch. Relate this back to the hadith above, and the importance of choosing good friends.

Activity 3: The "Shortcut of Love" Walk and Map

Choose a safe and relatively short walking path to go on a walk with the children. Create a simple map ahead of time with two different routes showing how to get to the same destination. One should be much shorter than the other. (Both should be pleasant paths, perhaps with the shorter one having something more special if possible.) Ask the children to examine the map and choose the best path to get them to their destination. Let the children know that this activity has a limited amount of time available for reaching the destination. Ask the children, "Which path will you choose to take to make it there on time?" If possible, allow the children to actually take their chosen paths and meet them at the destination.

Once congregated again, reflect on which path was best to get them to their destination within safe timing. Share with the children something similar to the following message in your own words: "The shortcut to a pure Spiritual Heart is having great love for the Messenger ﷺ because when you connect your heart to his ﷺ, you are connecting your heart to the most, sound pure heart of all. And when you love

The Book of the Mysteries of Purification For Children Workbook

the Messenger ﷺ with all of your heart, you will want to copy him ﷺ perfectly in both his outward and most importantly inward way of being."

Further develop this activity by providing artwork supplies to the children in order that they create their own Spiritual Heart Maps that demonstrate taking the path of great love for the Messenger ﷺ and seriously following his inward example versus just following outward Islamic rituals but not developing great love for the Messenger ﷺ and disregarding his ﷺ inward example.

Chapter Ten: Curriculum Guidance
Refer to recommended class schedule above in Curriculum Overview

Core Lesson: Wiping over your face and eyes brightens your face with Light.

Essential Question: What kinds of things should one look at and what should one avoid looking at? Why?

Definition Board: outline, eye sockets, demonstrate, measure, gloomy

Qur'an Passage related to Chapter Story: Ask a child to read aloud Surah 10 Verse 26 for everyone to copy into their workbooks during workbook time: "To those who do right is a goodly (reward) yea, more (than in measure)! No darkness nor shame shall cover their faces! They are Companions of the Garden; they will abide therein." Discuss.

Activity 1: *Wudu* Interactive Skit with Focus on the Eyes

Follow the directions for developing and performing interactive skits, but focus today's efforts on vices related to the eyes such as envy, spying, etc. Discuss how spying and envy can arise from sight. As with all interactive skits, the children should also demonstrate how to correct wrong ways of using one's eyes.

Activity 2: Smile Demonstration and Games

First, ask a child to read aloud the following *sahih* hadith: the Prophet Muhammad ﷺ said: "Every good deed is charity. Verily, it is a good deed to meet your brother with a smiling face, and to pour what is left from your bucket into the vessel of your brother." (Sunan At-Tirmidhi 1970)

Now, utilize "feelings" or emotions charts/flashcards to show different kinds of faces we can show to people and how our facial expressions influence other people. Let the children all put on moody, gloomy, sad, angry, etc. faces to demonstrate how awful these expressions are to behold. They will enjoy this while experiencing for themselves the effect of unpleasant facial appearances.

Next, describe to the children the beautiful smile of the Prophet Muhammad ﷺ! How did he make others feel around him with his beautiful smile, ﷺ? Emphasize making a habit of always smiling when greeting their teachers, parents, friend, siblings, etc. And even if not feeling well, it is important to greet everyone with a respectful tone of voice.

Suggested games:

A. Pair off for "smile contests" – whoever can smile the longest at another person wins a healthy treat. (Hint: Let everyone win a treat in the end so that the children's spirits remain high.)

B. Play "pass the smile" where everyone sits in a circle, and the first person smiles with the biggest smile they can to the person on their right and so on passing smiles all around.

Activity 3: Sparkling Smiley Faces for a Beloved Elder

Ask the children to think about how our elders might feel if they do not receive our frequent visits and attention. This craft will be given as a gift to special elders in the lives of the children. Make clear that you will be using glitter in this art project as a metaphor: glitter sticks to everything it comes in contact with just like how a radiant, shining face is contagious to others as well.

Materials you will need:
- Sturdy paper plates made from recycled sources
- Felt (various colors)
- Strong glue
- Glitter glue for decorating
- Buttons

Use the above materials to create a "sparkling smiley face" with the children's own inspirations. Attach a note containing the Prophet's ﷺ saying, "Every good deed is charity. Verily, it is a good deed to meet your brother with a smiling face" and explain the rationale for the artwork.

Chapter Eleven: Curriculum Guidance
Refer to recommended class schedule above in Curriculum Overview

Core Lesson: *Wudu* influences both this temporal world, and the eternal true life to come. In this world, *wudu* serves as a protection for us by helping us do good and avoid bad. In the Next World, a special Light will shine wherever the *wudu* water has reached on the body.

Essential Question: What kinds of things could *wudu* shield you from in this life? What could it help you achieve in the Next Life? What kind of a story could you write about your life in this process of purification?

Definition Board: Resurrection, splendorous, protection

Qur'an Passages related to Chapter Story: Ask a child to read aloud the verses mentioned in Chapter 11, including 84:07-15. Reflect on the passages and copy them into workbooks or journals:

"Then, he who is given his record in his right hand, soon will his account be taken as an easy reckoning, and he will turn to his people rejoicing! But he who has been given his record behind his back, soon he will cry for perdition, and will enter a blazing fire. Truly, did he go about among his people, rejoicing!? Truly did he think that he would not have to return (to Us)? Nay, nay! For his Lord was ever watchful of him."

The children could also act this out; doing so would support recollections of this verse.

Activity 1: Make a *Wudu* Shield

Brainstorm with the children about what kinds of things "*wudu* can shield us from." Ask the children to keep a list of five things they pray for *wudu* to protect them from.

Materials you will need:
- One or two pieces of strong cardboard
- A piece of string/rope/ribbon for the handle
- Pen
- Utility knife
- Large piece of paper
- Decoration suggestions – silver duct tape, paint/colored paper/felt/cloth pieces to cover majority of shield, glitter or glow-in-the dark glue for "spiritual hearts", markers to create their own Islamic calligraphy or print-outs to be pasted to shield

The Book of the Mysteries of Purification For Children Workbook

Note: Muslim shields were historically round, and covered in leather

Instructions:

1. To make a symmetric shield shape, first create a template with the large piece of paper. Fold the large piece of paper in half. Beginning from the fold line, draw a half circle. Cut and unfold the paper.

2. Use the paper template to trace the shape of the shield onto the two pieces of cardboard, one at a time.

3. An adult should use the utility knife to cut out the shapes of both cardboard pieces.

4. Choose one piece of circular cardboard to be the top and one to be the bottom. (You will use the silver tape to keep the two cardboard cut-outs together and to yield a stronger shield.)

5. To make a knight shield handle, cut two slits centered the in the middle of the shield. Both shields should have the slits in the same spots. Slide string/rope/ribbon through both holes and staple the ribbon in the back to make a closed loop.

6. Decorate the visible sides. On the front of the shield, calligraphy, spiritual hearts, etc. On the back of the shield, the children should write down their personal list of five things they pray for their *Wudu* Shield to protect them from.

7. Run the silver duct tape along the edge of both shields to tape them together.

Activity 3: My Life Book

In this craft, the children will learn an amazing truth about their lives: that everything they feel, think, and do is recorded in their "Life Book." Just like a famous author writes a compelling story that the reader loves to read, each of us is also trying to write an amazingly beautiful life story in our "Life Book."

Provide the children with folded together pieces of cardstock paper, construction paper, blank stationary, or blank children's books (which can be bought at craft stores or online). They may also use a page in their journal. The children will write the life story they would want Allah ﷻ to read about them. Depending on the age of the children, they may need one-on-one assistance to write in a story-like format.

The following is an example:

Maryam Noor was born on January 10th, 2004 to her mother and father. As a little girl she loved to... As she grew up she learned to..."help the poor by making food for them"..."always tell the truth"... Sometimes Maryam struggled because..."it was hard to share"..."other children teased her and she became upset"...but she learned to overcome this by..."loving to make other people happy"..."forgiving other people"...When she grew up she became a..."scholar of Islam"..."doctor"..."fireman"...She helped everyone around her by...She was known to be..."kind," "helpful," "humble." She lived her life in service of Allah ﷻ.

Activity 4: Children's Poem to accompany "My Life Book"

Incorporate poetry into your classroom by simply reading a poem to the children, writing it out beautifully on the cover of their "My Life Book" craft, or even having them memorize it. Shaykh Abdal Hakim Murad has published a fantastic children's book with classical Islamic poetry for children entitled *Montmorency's Book of Rhymes*. Simply read the poem below and attribute it to the author (from p. 93 of the book):

"In Allah's ﷻ great Book, where but angels look
On pages of spotless beauty,
Are written in letters of living light
A Muslim's life and his duty"

A Parent-Teacher's Manual of Activities and Curriculum

Chapter Twelve: Curriculum Guidance
Refer to recommended class schedule above in Curriculum Overview

Core Lesson: The wiping of the top of the head and neck reminds us of being in the merciful shade of God's ﷻ throne in the Next World.

Essential Question: When you wipe your ears, what help do you ask from Allah ﷻ?

Definition Board: demonstrate, separate, amusing, counsel (not to be confused with 'council')

Qur'an Passage related to Chapter Story:

Ask a child to read aloud the following hadith during workbook time: "In Paradise, there is a tree under the shadow of which a rider can travel for a hundred years." Discuss and copy into workbooks.

Variation for *Wudu* Contemplation Time: While wiping hands over head and neck, everyone should say together three times: "O Allah, cover me with Your Mercy, send down upon me Your blessings and shade me in the shade of Your Throne on the Day when there is no shade except Your shade."

While wiping their hands over their ears, everyone should say together three times Surah 39 Verse 18: "Whoever listens to speech and follows the best of it… those are the ones God has guided, and those are people of understanding."

Activity 1: Shade as A Sign of Allah ﷻ

Take the children outside on a sunny day, preferably when it is hot. Ask them to describe what it feels like and to imagine how hot it could be on Judgement Day. Then take them to the shade of a tree or open an umbrella for them. Ask them to describe how much better they feel. Then tell them that the cool shade that Allah ﷻ will provide will be infinitely better. Remind them to think about this when wiping the tops of their heads during *wudu*. Then write the following prayer on the board and ask the children to reflect upon it: "O Allah, cover me with Your Mercy, send down upon me Your blessings and shade me in the shade of Your Throne on the Day when there is no shade except Your shade."

Activity 2: Positive versus Negative Thinking

Provide modeling clay or homemade play dough for the children. Ask each child to think of a situation they are struggling with. In relation to this situation, ask the children to think of one scenario that contains virtues (and is overall positive) and one that contains vices (and is overall negative). This may require one on one time with children to help them think through the scenarios. After, ask the children to use the clay/dough to create a shape that represents their negative scenario. How do they feel about it? Is it ugly?

Now they can flatten the "negative thought," and reshape it into something that symbolizes the positive scenario. Discuss with the children how this relates to negative and positive thinking, and how thinking relates to our emotions and actions.

Chapter Thirteen: Curriculum Guidance
Refer to recommended class schedule above in Curriculum Overview

Core Lesson: Upon completing *wudu*, there is a prayer to be said which will rise up along with the shahada to beneath Allah's ﷻ throne, where it will continue to glorify Him and will also be there among your good deeds, waiting for you after your death. Discuss its meaning.

Essential Question: What can you ask God ﷻ to help you with as you walk or run?

Definition Board: bare, artistic, illustration, contentment, admit, repentance

Hadith related to Chapter Story: Ask a child to read aloud the following hadith during workbook time:

The Book of the Mysteries of Purification For Children Workbook

Anas said, "The Prophet ﷺ said, "Don't you think that for every step of yours (that you take towards the mosque) there is a reward (while coming for prayer)?"

Discuss and copy into workbooks.

Variation for *Wudu* Contemplation Time: First, post the recommended prayer in an area that everyone can see: "O God, I turn to You in repentance so forgive me and accept my repentance. You truly are the Forgiving and the Compassionate! O God, make me among those who turn to You in repentance, and make me among those who purify themselves, and make me among Your righteous servants, and make me Your patient and grateful servant, among those who invoke You much and glorify You early and late."

After completing the *wudu* contemplation ritual, read the above *dua'a* slowly. After every few words, ask the children to try say it in their own words. Write out examples of the children's interpretations on the board.

Activity 1: Feet Tracing Art Memorable

Materials you will need:
- Construction paper
- Glitter Glue
- Water paint/markers/colored pencils
- Decorative paper for border

The purpose of this activity is to learn a sunnah of the Beloved Prophet ﷺ. Stress this point to the children so as to not undermine its deeper meaning. Play Islamic songs honoring the Prophet ﷺ in the background as the children complete this activity.

Lead the children through the activity that Haj Abdullah describes in the story. The children will trace around their right and left feet so that each toe is clearly visible. Getting into work pairs will make this task easier. Then have them number their toes starting with the right pinky toe (#1) and ending with the left pinky toe (#10). Explain that this is the order in which they should be washing their toes when washing their feet during *wudu*. Provide art materials so that they can decorate their feet tracings, and keep them for reference. Date the front of the drawing so that it can also be used as a memorable item for children and parents.

Activity 2: Make Booklet *Wudu* Guidance/Reminder Cards

Laminate the *Wudu* Guidance/Reminder cards or apply contact paper so that they can be kept near the sink and quickly reviewed before performing *wudu*. Now that the end of the program is approaching, ask the children to gather all the cards they have used throughout the program. Punch a hole into the *Wudu* Guidance/Reminder Cards and connect them all with a card ring. Add a front and back card that the children can decorate and personalize. This will become the children's own personal booklet. Please see www.ghazalichildren.org for a free printable of all the prophetic *dua'a*s.

Activity 3: Walk the Path of Gratitude

Begin this lesson with a simple game to demonstrate how unaware human beings are of all the blessings they have been given in life, and how choosing to be grateful is not only the right thing to do, but brings more happiness into one's life. Suggested games:

- Blindfold one child at a time and ask him/her to list out all they can remember about the details of their current surroundings. The child will be able to describe some, but not all of the details of the room. Discuss with the children how this example relates to gratitude (we are limited in how much we recognize/remember, there is an unseen world, etc.)

A Parent-Teacher's Manual of Activities and Curriculum

- Direct the children in making two columns on a piece of paper by drawing a line down the middle. Label the first column "Things I give to others" and the second column "Things that are Given to Me." The second column should include things that seem to be coming from other human beings and things that are more clearly from Allah ﷻ (although you could discuss how everything ultimately comes from Allah ﷻ). Discuss with the children how this example relates to how we all usually fall short in being grateful enough for all of our blessings.

- Remind the children about one of Imam al-Ghazali's stories in his *Book of Knowledge* about thankfulness. Let one child pretend to be a scary lion which escapes from the zoo and is trying to gobble up all the other children who play-act running away in fright. One child turns and boldly drives the bad lion away, and everyone thanks the child for saving their lives. Then let another child pretend he is a grandfather or elder who is passing on spiritual teaching which can save the children's lives in this world. Shouldn't the children be even more grateful to their teacher or elder who passes on the Real Special Learning of how to polish the Heart?

During class time or out of class, ask the children to choose a time in their day to begin a habit of thinking of three things they are grateful for, and thanking Allah ﷻ for them. Explain that the practice of gratitude will make them stronger to do the work of cleaning their spiritual hearts and performing the ritual practices of Islam.

The teacher can open www.ghazalichildren.org to the "My Blessings" activity. Together the class will suggest blessings and take turns adding them to the website.

Chapter Fourteen: Curriculum Guidance
Refer to recommended class schedule above in Curriculum Overview

Core Lesson: The inward aspect of *wudu* is essential.

Essential Question: Why is thoughtlessly rushing through the body movements of *wudu* not good enough?

Definition Board: thoughtful, efforts, wasting, rubbish, symbolize

Qur'an Passages related to Chapter Story: Ask a child to read aloud part of Surah 23 Verse 116 during workbook time: "Now Allah be Exalted, the True King! There is no God save Him, the Lord of the Throne of Grace." Then, read aloud part of Surah 64 Verse 4: "He knows what is in the heavens and on earth; and He knows what ye conceal and what ye reveal: yea, God knows well the (secrets) of (all) hearts."

Discuss the implication of these verses with the children and ask how they can understand them in the context of their lives. Copy passages into workbooks.

Activity 1: Preparing for the Royal Visit Mini-Play

Review the story of the king's visit in the chapter. Share the following hadith with the children as a guide for this activity: "God does not consider your forms nor your wealth, rather He considers your hearts and your actions." (Muslim)

Bring a cardboard box to class from which children can create a small house. At first, ask the children to collect dirt and trash and throw it inside the box. The children receive a message that a great king or queen is coming to visit the house and intends to stay as a guest. Hearing this, the children forget about the inside of the house full of dirt and trash, and begin to spend a lot of time and effort using colorful markers to decorate the outside of the house with a beautiful door, windows and shutters, bushes, and flowers.

Next, one child pretends to be a king or queen who has come to visit. The king/queen makes a simple compliment on the appearance of the outside of the house and immediately goes to open the door. When

The Book of the Mysteries of Purification For Children Workbook

s/he opens the door, s/he is horrified. The rest of the children, who live inside this home, are very embarrassed and try to apologize.

The king/queen decides to give the children time to clean the inside of the home. The children clean inside, and explain to the king/queen how this relates to the inner *wudu*. Now, the king/queen is pleased to enter.

After performing the mini-play, discuss the following questions with the children:

1. In relation to the above hadith, what does the outside of the house and the inside of the house symbolize?
2. What was the king/queen most interested in?
3. What does the king/queen's visit symbolize?
4. How does this example relate to *wudu*?

Please send photos/videos of this activity to ghazalichildren.org. Other children will love this!

Chapter Fifteen: Curriculum Guidance
Refer to recommended class schedule above in Curriculum Overview

Core Lesson: More blessings occur when one does extra *rakah*s, concentrates well, or does *wudu* in difficult circumstances. There are many extra ways of polishing the heart in *wudu*.

Essential Question: What happens if you renew your *wudu* even when it is not broken?

Definition Board: simmered, *rakah*, renewed, stunned

Qur'an Passage related to Chapter Story: Ask a child to read aloud part of Surah 3 Verse 191 during workbook time: "Such as remember Allah, standing, sitting, and reclining, and consider the creation of the heavens and the earth, (and say): Our Lord! Thou createst not this in vain. Glory be to Thee! Preserve us from the doom of Fire."

Talk about ways of remembering God ﷻ and why God ﷻ created the world.

Variation for *Wudu* Contemplation Time: Go to a basin where children can perform the *wudu* they have now learned. Ask each child to concentrate on and choose one place - eyes, nose, mouth, face, ears, hands, or feet which they especially want to cleanse of bad deeds. As they think deeply about it, ask the children to notice their physical and emotional experience. What did they notice while performing *wudu* with concentration?

Activity 1: *Wudu* Before We Sleep Learning Experience

Make a fun, scheduled event to practice making *wudu* before the children go to sleep. Serve a special snack before sleeping and tell an extra story or sing an extra song. Remind them of all the blessings of going to sleep pure and of having said the shahada after every ablution. Right before sleeping, ask the children to think about something they want God's ﷻ help with (ideally something non-materialistic). Earlier in the day, each child should write his/her *dua'a* on a piece of paper, fold it, and keep it underneath his/her pillow. When they are in bed, ask them to shut their eyes and imagine their glowing hearts. Try to establish this act as a ritual beginning with once a month and eventually moving to once a week, and then eventually nightly.

Activity 2: Sing "An Islamic Lullaby"

The Fons Vitae website includes a link to a beautiful Islamic Lullaby: https://ghazalichildren.org/things-to-do/an-islamic-lullaby-sing-along/.

Lyrics are shown on the video. Sing during class time and also before bed.

A Parent-Teacher's Manual of Activities and Curriculum

Chapter Sixteen: Curriculum Guidance
Refer to recommended class schedule above in Curriculum Overview

Core Lesson: If we see something beautiful, it can recall Paradise, our true goal. We should also act with beauty and be noble and dignified in appearance.

Essential Question: What are some things people do that you find beautiful?

Definition Board: situation, admire, casual, dignified, impress

Hadith Passage related to Chapter Story: Ask a child to read aloud the following hadith during workbook time: Abdullah ibn Mas'ud *radiallahu 'anhu* reported that the Prophet *sallallahu 'alayhi wa salam* said, "No one will enter Paradise who has an atom's weight of pride in his heart." A man said, "What if a man likes his clothes to look good and his shoes to look good?" He said, "Allah is beautiful and loves beauty. Pride means denying the truth and looking down on people." (Muslim)

Discuss pride with the children and ask them for examples. Copy the hadith into workbooks.

Activity 1: Beauty Magazine Collage

Ask the children to brainstorm about created things that are beautiful in this world, and which remind them of heaven.

Provide a variety of magazines (be weary of questionable material), and ask the children to search for examples to cut out. Create individual or one large class mural(s). Ask the children to imagine how much greater heaven will be and to try to describe it. Every time the children come to a point in their imagination, smilingly say "Oh, it is even better than that." The goal is to try to come to a point of complete awe with the children at the thought of the "beauty of heaven beyond imagination."

Activity 2: *Wudu* Interactive Skits with a Focus on "Ugly Truths"

Share the following script with the children to describe the focus of the *Wudu* Interactive Skits for this chapter:

Truth is beautiful, but Imam al-Ghazali taught us that there are *ugly* truths. What could these be? Maybe you tell everyone about someone important you know or about a new toy or computer you got. Even though what you say is true, you mention them to brag – to "one-up" others. Another ugly truth would be to point out that your friend's shoes are falling apart or that someone does not bring much for lunch; these may be true, but they make others feel bad and can even be a form of bragging.

Ask each child to act out saying two ugly truths someone might say.

Activity 3: Humility is the Key Virtue Demonstration

Materials you will need:
- Strong white string for humility
- Five or more large colored beads
  - Red for generosity
  - Green for patience
  - Blue for kindness
  - Yellow for not speaking badly about anyone
  - Orange for honesty

1. Discuss the meaning of each craft item with the children.

2. Ask the children to string all the beads onto the string and make a loose tie that you will call the "knot of humility."

3. Now untie the string and hold up the string. (All of the beads should fall to the floor.)

4. Ask the children, "What happened to all of your virtues when the knot of humility was opened and the string of humility which held them all together, on which they *depended*, was pulled out?"

5. Talk about each bead and what happens to its virtue – like kindness or generosity – if you are proud and full of yourself and not humble. What would honesty or kindness actually be like? Try to act these out – being kind and not humble. Does it work?

6. Re-string the beads and allow the children to keep their bracelets if not needed for another class. Let them illustrate the lesson to their family members.

Chapter Seventeen: Curriculum Guidance
Refer to recommended class schedule above in Curriculum Overview

Core Lesson: The order in which we do the rites in Islam – like *wudu* and prayer – relates to how the Messenger did these acts of worship. Following him in his outward actions reminds us to follow him in his inward actions (virtues). The "My Shining Heart Program" will conclude by emphasizing love for the Prophet Muhammad by following both his outward and inward *sunnah*, or example.

Essential Question: What does following the "path of Muhammad " mean to me?

Definition Board: trim, noble, index finger, demonstrate, regularly, cautiously, standard, haphazard, rhythmically, norm

Qur'an Passage related to Chapter Story: Assign a child the reading aloud of part of Surah 4 Verse 59 during workbook time: "O ye who believe! Obey God, and obey the Apostle, and those charged with authority among you. If ye differ in anything among yourselves, refer it to God and His Apostle, if ye do believe in God and the Last Day: That is better and fairer in outcome." Discuss and copy into notebook.

Activity 1: Hand and Feet Art Memorables

Materials you will need:
- Construction paper
- Glitter Glue
- Water paint/markers/colored pencils
- Decorative paper for border

The purpose of this activity is to learn a sunnah of the Beloved Prophet . Stress this point to the children so as to not undermine its deeper meaning. Play Islamic songs honoring the Prophet in the background as the children complete this activity.

Group the children into pairs to trace each other's hands and feet. The children will create a visual for learning the order in which fingernails and toenails are clipped. After tracing a picture of each hand onto paper, number the right index finger #1, and continue the numbering to the right. The left pinky finger will be #5 and the right thumb will be #10.

Using the artwork from "Chapter 13, Activity 1: Feet Tracing Art Memorable" or by creating a new tracing, re-number the toes in the order in which toenails are clipped. Begin with the right big toe as #1. Then moving to the right, number each toe. Once the right foot is complete, start with the left pinky toe as #6 and move to the right, ending with the left big toe as #10.

A Parent-Teacher's Manual of Activities and Curriculum

Activity 2: Following the Prophet's ﷺ Inward Example – Guess Who? Virtue Game

Explain to the children that part of today's class time will be used to reflect on the inner virtues of our Beloved Prophet ﷺ. It may be useful to share the Core Lesson for Chapter 17. The virtue "patience" has been chosen because it was a great virtue of the Prophet Muhammad ﷺ, and the children will need it to keep up their hard work in practicing Islamic rites and developing good character. Do not let the children know that the theme is "patience" until after they have completed the "Guess Who? Virtue Game." But list five virtues on the board for them to be considering as the poem is read.

Give a copy of the poem below to the children. You can copy from this book or go to the www.ghazalichildren.org and copy/paste from the online curriculum.

Who Am I?

Hello, I am your friend and have a name, can you guess who I am?
Some people push me away
because they don't think I'm fun.
But those who know me,
find out that I'm a very helpful friend.

People who want everything their way don't like me.
But, people who trust in Allah ﷻ like me and rely on me.
I help my friends get rid of mean feelings
so they can see their own beautiful hearts.

If you stay close to me
I also help you to be calm when
other people act nasty or mean to you.

Those who love me know that
everything is in Allah's hands ﷻ
and that they can always depend on Him ﷻ.
This helps them to feel calm when troubles come.

Never forget to bring me with you
wherever you go.
I will make you strong
and light your way.

I am easy to love.
If you hold onto me
I can be your loyal friend.

My dear ones,
look inside your heart,
see that I am actually,
part of what you truly are.

Activity 3: Friends of Patience Speak Mini-Play or Artwork

Ask the children to read the below poem which represents the relationship that patience has to other

The Book of the Mysteries of Purification For Children Workbook

virtues. Provide any necessary materials for the children to develop a creative mini-play or artwork to demonstrate these relationships.

Friends of Patience Speak

Mercy says: "When I teach you how to forgive, I work closely with Patience."
Intelligence says: "Patience is practical and all those who like me, like Patience."
Courage says: "Together Patience and I destroy fear."
Love says: "Patience is one of my best friends. Any friend of Patience is a friend of mine too."

Activity 4: "Patience in My Life" Personal Reflection Time for Journal

Create a relaxing setting for the children to spend quiet time writing in their journals. If not disrupting, quietly play Islamic songs honoring the Prophet ﷺ in the background as the children complete this activity. Guide the children through this reflection exercise with the following prompts. Write them on the board so that the children can copy them into their journals:

1. When I am patient, I feel…

2. Patience makes my life...

3. No matter how bad I feel, patience helps me…

The children should complete each prompt in their journal. Here are examples that you can use to guide the children or show them at the end of the exercise. However, it is important to give the children time to critically think about patience before giving them an answer.

1. When I am patient, I feel strong and wise.

2. Patience makes life easier and brings me peace.

3. No matter how bad I feel, patience helps me trust that everything will be okay.

Now ask the children to quietly brainstorm some examples from their daily lives when it would be very useful to practice patience. Below is a list of examples. Share a few with the children before they begin to brainstorm, but postpone sharing the whole list until they have created their own ideas:

- When we need to pay close attention to our homework or any kind work, patience is helpful.

- If our car ride or bus ride seems slow, patience makes the ride more fun.

- Learning new things can be stressful. When we breathe deeply and feel patience, it makes learning easier.

- Listening more and talking less helps us to have patience with friends and family.

- If we have to wait for something we really want, patience makes us strong and helps us wait.

- Patience can make it easier to share.

- When we feel worried, patience helps us to get rid of fear, because we know Allah ﷻ is taking care of everything and He knows best.

- Those that have physical or mental problems feel better when the people around them act patiently and with true care.

- Patience helps us understand that not everyone thinks as we do.

- Being patient with yourself when you make mistakes helps you to be patient with others when they make mistakes. Patience blesses us and it blesses others too.

And God, glory be to He, is with the patient ones.

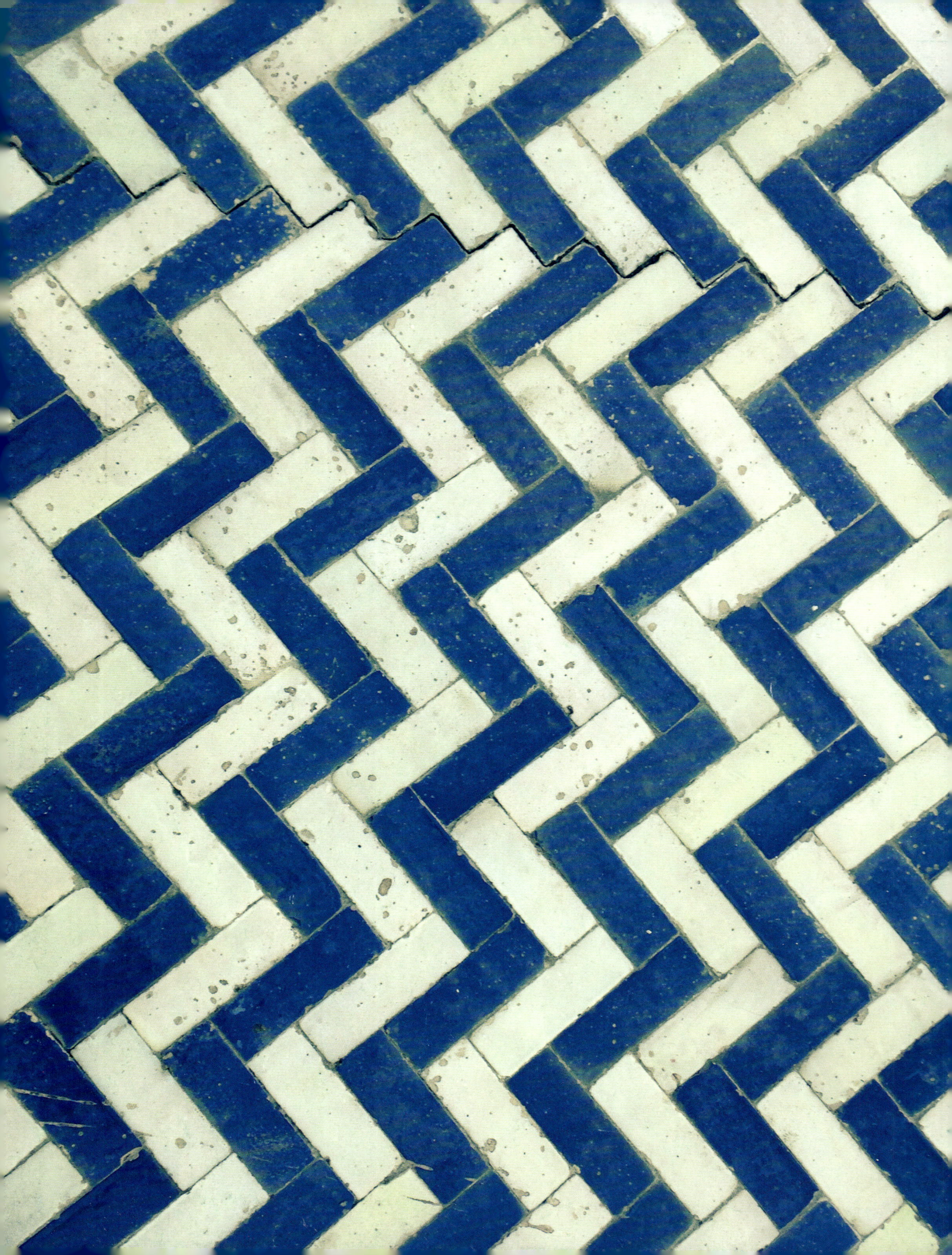